DESIGNING STRATEGY

DESIGNING STRATEGY

a how-to book
for managers

GEORGE C. SAWYER

JOHN WILEY & SONS
New York • Chichester • Brisbane • Toronto • Singapore

Library of Congress Cataloging in Publication Data:

Sawyer, George C.
  Designing strategy.

Includes index.
  1. Strategic planning.   I. Title.
HD30.28.S282 1985   658.4'012   85-17815
ISBN 0-471-81682-5

Printed in the United States of America

10 9 8 7 6 5 4 3 2 1

To
Margo

PREFACE

This book discusses business strategy in terms of two sets of ideas that link planning and strategy to action. At the working level key elements fit together into a product or business strategy. However, all of these strategies are governed by limits that management sets for the enterprise as a whole—almost like commandments—often as an incidental by-product of day-to-day decisions. A product or business strategy can be described in terms of a few key elements and the 10 commandments that govern its function.

The strategy determines the scope and effectiveness of the resources of a business. At the start investors provide capital, but the organization's capabilities and market franchises quickly become major assets and often determine the relative availability of other resources. An initial basis for business strategy was a set of principles defined from classic military campaigns. However, business strategy is more complex because there are more possible courses of action than there were for Robert E. Lee or Napoleon. And where military strategy builds on the best use of available resources, in business situations many of the most important resources are created by the strategy as a means to the desired accomplishments.

By devising a strategy based on new approaches to the conduct of its business management can bypass and outdistance competitors. Strategy is based on simple ideas combined effectively. The science of strategy is in knowing which combinations to explore, and the art of strategic management is in selecting those that can be put into action successfully.

The ideas behind strategy and its design have long since been translated into business terms. Yet business strategy is not a clearly defined subject. The difficulty is that the first good books, such as Igor Ansoff's *Corporate Strategy* twenty years ago,[1] stimulated ideas so diverse that the field was fragmented. The good result was a rapid expansion of writing and research resulting in a wide variety of new ideas and findings. Interesting practical approaches include those from General Electric, the Boston Consulting Group, Arthur D. Little, and McKinsey & Co.

As each new aspect of business strategy has been recognized, the tendency has been to elaborate it separately as a new branch of investigation. The consequence has been to make the central ideas more obscure. Ouchi's Theory Z, Hofer's refinements of portfolio analysis, Quinn's logical incrementalism, Pascale and Athos's presentation of the McKinsey 7S framework, Peters and Waterman's characterization of excellent companies, Porter's competitive strategies, and Ohmae's stress on the key factors for success—these are not so much competitive developments as important thrusts, each at a different portion of the frontier.

There has been a minimum of effective central integration of this field. Under the impact of this new knowledge the field of strategy has become more and more challenging for the beginner. Worse still, it has become less accessible to those who design and apply strategy because most managers lack the time to study overlaps and conflicts between different strategy concepts.

Purpose and Plan

Business strategy has a simple core. The purpose of this book is to present it in a way that will show a newcomer to the field or a busy

[1]H. Igor Ansoff, *Corporate Strategy* (New York: McGraw-Hill, 1965).

manager its logic, to develop an understanding that will permit practical strategy design. Many of the ideas presented are drawn from the mass of earlier good work in the field; others were developed here or in *Corporate Planning as a Creative Process,*[2] or *Business and Its Environment.*[3]

The sort of strategy that makes money for a company starts with a customer's need and satisfies that need, whether this requires a lower product cost, improvements in product function or quality, or a more ingenious marketing presentation. However, strategy is also set by the managers' decisions about the sort of business they want and how it will run, because this determines how well certain customer needs can be filled.

Designing Strategy is built around the basic linkages from planning and strategy to action, as illustrated on page x, and the fundamentals on which this flow depends. The book begins with the resource creation process as basic to successful business strategy, with the essential mission and the way management must make up its own rules for the business it operates. From this the book moves to goals, policies, and strategies, and defines the different strategy levels—enterprise strategy which fixes the framework, and business and product strategy by which it is executed.

Any strategy needs support, three-cornered support in this case, in the basics of product, market, and business. It must also be put into action by an organization, and a review of the action requirements leads to the definition of an excellence model for meeting high organizational performance requirements.

The next step is to needs-leverages linkages and the process of business and product strategy design. Strategic blindness causes fatal errors; ways of avoiding it are outlined, as are essential processes of strategic control. The organization needs an opportunity management process, a plan for its people and operations, and a built-in renewal process. These discussions lay

[2]George C. Sawyer, *Corporate Planning as a Creative Process* (Oxford, Ohio: Planning Executives Institute, 1983).

[3]George C. Sawyer, *Business and its Environment* (Englewood Cliffs, N.J.: Prentice-Hall, 1985).

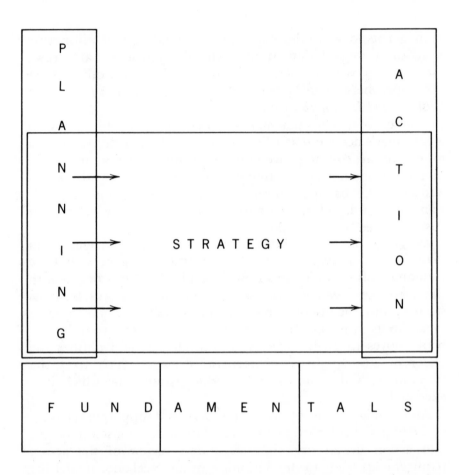

the groundwork for a restatement of the underlying concepts of strategy design, the boundaries that establish how good a strategy must be, and the importance of rent collecting. Next come the sources of power for a strategy, the essence of this power creation, and the endpoint: strategies leading to profits because they fill the needs better.

Perspective

This book is divided into five sections. Part 1, **Policy, Strategy, and the Business Firm,** develops the basic framework of business strategies after a discussion of the mission and goals on which they depend. Part 2, **Foundations for Strategy,** presents the elements of a product or service strategy and then basic product, market, and business characteristics that govern strategy design. Part 3, **Designing Effective Strategies,** discusses the organizational requirements of certain strategies and how to achieve them, the strategy design process, and the risk of errors due to strategic blindness. Part 4, **Strategic Action and Control,** develops in more detail a number of the necessary management processes underlying sound enterprise strategy and its translation to action. Part 5, **Practicing Strategic Management,** summarizes some of the key considerations in strategy design and that translation to action.

GEORGE C. SAWYER

Garrison, New York
July 1985

CONTENTS

an enterprise—enterprise choice criteria: desirability, managing, belonging, credibility, and payoff strategies; choice strategies—summary: enterprise strategies and achievement strategies.

PART 2   FOUNDATIONS FOR STRATEGY

PART 3 DESIGNING EFFECTIVE STRATEGIES

PART 4 STRATEGIC ACTION AND CONTROL

PART 5   PRACTICING STRATEGIC MANAGEMENT

DESIGNING
STRATEGY

PART 1

Policy, Strategy and the Business Firm

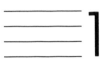

MAKING UP RULES
AND CREATING RESOURCES

This book is about strategies and how to design them. The basics of strategy design are relatively simple. The purpose here is to present these basics to help those who design strategy do it better and to help others learn.

Before discussing strategy design it is important to be clear on what a strategy is and how it relates to the business or other organization in which it is used. This first chapter describes the nature and role of a business, the way in which mission and goals precede strategies, and the freedom and need executives have to make up new rules, and to create many of the resources necessary to allow their strategies to succeed.

THE MISSION OR SOCIAL ROLE

A business exists for a purpose—for a social role or mission—because its continuation depends on making a profit. Profit can be earned only if the business sells goods or services for more than they cost to produce. This means that the goods or services must have a sufficient value to the customers to justify a price that will result in a profit. Otherwise the purchasers will spend their money on something else and the business will cease to exist.

A mission of a specific business is its purpose, the specific set of society's needs that the business seeks to satisfy. Society, and the individuals of which it is comprised, will pay to satisfy its needs, therefore a firm that is defining a social role is establishing a potential equation. It hopes to earn a profit by filling those needs for a cost less than it is able to charge. The social role becomes a hunting license for a territory within which management hopes to generate a profit (Figure 1.1).

Newman and Logan[1] and Ackoff et al.[2] relate mission to a much broader statement of purpose, but although their examples are crisp and concise many of the statements developed with this approach by others become general listings of what the organization hopes to be like in a variety of social and operational dimensions. The results are too non-specific to form bases for concrete programs.

By narrowing the purpose to the specific social role the organization seeks to fulfill, a tighter, more concrete base for action is created. It is much easier to create and maintain a close-to-the-customer, market-driven organization if the mission is designed specifically to satisfy customer needs, with goals defined within the scope of this mission and a strategy aimed at progress toward those goals.

To restate. The mission of a business is the social role it will fulfill

---

[1] William H. Newman and James P. Logan, *Strategy, Policy and Central Management*, 8th ed. (Cincinnati: South-Western, 1981).

[2] Russell L. Ackoff, Elsa Vergara Finnel, and Jamshid Gharajedaghi, *A Guide to Controlling Your Corporation's Future* (New York: Wiley, 1984).

Where to hunt for profits?

Figure 1.1. The mission or social role.

by satisfying certain needs of customers or society well enough to ensure that these customers will pay more for the goods or services than it costs the business to deliver them.

GOALS AND STRATEGIES

The goals of an organization are the targets within the area defined by its mission. Goals and objectives are treated here as roughly equivalent, although goals are more likely to be larger or longer term and the specific and short-term are more likely to be called objectives in the "management-by-objectives" sense. The mission provides the framework, the goals define targets within the mission, which, when achieved, should move the organization toward the performance of that mission, and the strategies are the basis for action plans aimed at achieving the goals.

A BUSINESS AS A CORPORATION

The large majority of businesses function as corporations. A corporation is an economic entity made possible by law. In a famous Supreme Court decision Chief Justice John Marshall wrote:

> *A corporation is an artificial being, invisible, intangible, and existing only in contemplation of the law. Being the mere creature of the law, it possesses only those properties which the charter of its creation confers upon it. . . . Among the most important are immortality and . . . individuality; properties by which a perpetual succession of many persons are considered the same, and may act as a single individual.*[3]

The importance of this definition is the emphasis on the corporation as an artificial creature of the law, limited by its charter and the laws that govern it. The corporation has a legal framework that is also economic in nature. Survival requires economic performance and the corporation is conditioned to react in an economic dimension.

It has been said that money is the language of the firm. Essentially all significant businesses are corporations, and corporations by their nature must behave according to economic constraints. Yet many of the considerations that influence management actions are social and ethical in nature and are often difficult to accommodate within an economic framework. There is an inherent contradiction here. Even in charitable and other not-for-profit corporations the basically economic nature of the legal structure often causes conflict with the social purpose or mission of the organization.

ACHIEVING SOCIAL ENDS BY ECONOMIC MEANS

The mission is a social role, but the firm is an economic entity whose survival depends on economic performance. It spite of the inherent conflict between its social purpose and its economic

---

[3]The Trustees of Dartmouth College versus Woodward, *4 Wheat.* (U.S.) 518, 636 (1819).

nature, the business strives for social ends by economic means. If a business sells those quantities of its products that are necessary to achieve a level of economic performance sufficient for survival and growth, those products must be—as evidenced by the continuing purchase—sufficiently beneficial to society. Given the fact of the purchase as an endorsement of the value of the product, the business is making a social contribution as well as an economic profit.

This argument assumes that society regulates the marketplace well enough to ensure that the products contain the value on which the customers base their continuing purchase, and that purchase of the product by customers is evidence of product worth.

Although our society attempts to restrict the sale of illegal products and to protect customers against deception and fraud, it also endorses a system by which product value (or service value) is a matter of individual decision rather than collective judgment. The sale of tobacco products, alcoholic beverages, adult literature, and firearms continues to be strongly opposed by significant elements in society, but the overall social judgment has been that the purchase endorsement of these products by specific customer groups justifies their existence, even in the face of intense disapproval by others. Society's position is that any legal product that is not misrepresented or defective in some way is a good product if people want to buy it; therefore a business makes a social contribution by supplying that product.

SCOPE OF THE MISSION

The mission of a business is to satisfy a specific type or class of customer need; that is its social role. Mission statements, as need-oriented and market-connected, tend to describe only one sort of business or relationship and often are so specific to an individual business that an enterprise consisting of several different businesses has difficulty in stating a mission that unifies them.

The scope of a mission statement is defined by the range of

needs that a business finds it practical to attempt to serve. Often the missions of a group of related businesses can be unified into a single statement that will cover all of them, and a conglomerate can be defined as a multibusiness enterprise without a single mission to unify the thrust of its members. This characteristic makes a conglomerate somewhat more difficult to manage and it loses some of the potential for synergism.[4]

WHAT RULES SHOULD THE BUSINESS RUN BY?

Management of a business enterprise—of an economic entity that is attempting to make profits and survive by achieving a social purpose—establishes rules of behavior as a part of its function of directing the enterprise. A striking difference between a corporation as an individual created by law and all other types of individual is that they are born into a social framework that lays down rules for individual behavior. In many human societies the rules are so detailed that a person could go through life by following them with almost no need for individual thought or decision. The corporate society, however, has no rules of this kind, beyond the bare requirements for filing certain reports and paying taxes.

Society has created "Thou shalt not!" rules to prevent price fixing and other disapproved business behavior but provides almost no positive guidance. The management of each corporation must create and establish its own set of rules of behavior, and, although it may choose to follow a general pattern, strict imitation of other businesses is usually unwise.

Management has the responsibility for studying the needs of its own specific business in the light of the mission it has selected and the competition it faces and devising rules for its operation that will yield satisfactory results. This task is never complete because the business never ceases to change and its problems and challenges continue to evolve. As new situations develop, new rules are

---

[4]For further discussion of the mission of a diverse enterprise see George C. Sawyer, *Corporate Planning as a Creative Process* (Oxford, Ohio: Planning Executives Institute, 1983), pp. 20–28.

required. Management must create them, must make them up as they are needed.

Business is always competitive, currently or potentially. As one management faces new situations and makes up new rules by which to operate, the managements of its competitors are doing the same. To the extent that business can be visualized as a competitive game, it is a game in which each player establishes its own rules within a framework established by law. Therefore those that are most ingenious in creating new rules are likely to achieve the best profits.

When Thomas J. Watson of IBM began to lease systems of office equipment in the 1920s,[5] as opposed to selling individual machines as his competitors did, he created a new market environment in which IBM customers no longer had equipment financing problems or risked their capital by investing it in business machines. IBM representatives designed the installation to fit the business needs and then helped with the startup. IBM service kept the system running and the customer business was assured of an operating system tailored to its needs; there was no investment— only a monthly fee.

No one else sold equipment this way, and IBM's competitors didn't seem to know how to respond as IBM steadily increased its market share. Watson made up new rules for office equipment marketing, made these rules effective through the supporting organization he built, and benefited greatly at the expense of his competitors. Because Watson was so much better at making up new rules than anyone else in that market place at that time, IBM began to grow toward that preeminence it has enjoyed ever since.

BUSINESS POLICIES

The rules that management sets for itself become policies. When management has selected a mission or social role, it then chooses specific targets or goals within that mission and focuses the energy and resources of the organization toward those goals by the

---

[5]Robert Sobel, *IBM: Colossus in Transition* (New York: Bantam Books, 1981), pp. 91–110.

strategy it defines. That strategy or general plan of action is put into effect by laying out guidelines for the action. These guidelines are policies, the rules for conduct of the business previously discussed.

This book deals with the process by which strategy is set and the pattern of conduct is defined in the areas of action in which the organization is enagaged. This process is most effective when its components are considered explicitly, but the ingredients of any pattern of management action implicitly generate similar rules. Any business will have a strategy and rules of conduct for the enterprise as a whole as well as for specific areas within it. Strategy is defined and policy is established by management decisions for research, capital expenditures, hiring and firing, pay increases, and the multitude of other actions necessary as an organization conducts its business and deals with the outside world.

CREATING RESOURCES

A part of strategy is the wise use of available resources. The art in games such as checkers and chess is to use those resources skillfully. As in most military strategy, the objective is to win by defeating a specific opponent. In game theory terminology these are largely zero-sum games. One player wins and the other loses.

Business strategy is different because neither the resource pool nor the payoffs are clearly delineated in advance. The competitive process is often a personal one, sometimes involving several players, and one or all of the players can augment his or her resource pool by a properly selected strategy and confront the others more effectively.

Peters and Waterman[6] used the Frito-Lay distribution system as an example of organizational excellence. Others also have praised this system. Frito-Lay built and trained a distribution team to an unusual level of effectiveness in support of the retailers. It created this resource as a part of its strategy for rapid growth in snack foods

[6] Thomas J. Peters and Robert H. Waterman, Jr., *In Search of Excellence: Lessons from America's Best-Run Companies* (New York: Harper & Row, 1982).

in the same way that IBM service was a necessary resource created by Watson to make possible the success cited earlier.

Forbes recently profiled Time Energy Systems,[7] a fast-growing service company that specialized in energy-saving control of heating and air conditioning in large buildings. Time Energy Systems liked to sell "free" control systems in which there was no up-front cost to the building owner and took a share of the energy savings as its profit. This method produced a profitable and a capital-hungry growth plan. David Brown, the founder, was fresh from bankruptcy of an unsuccessful startup company in a different field. How did a newly bankrupt entrepreneur get startup capital? Much of the early growth was funded by limited partnerships created building by building as the company grew, each secured by the contract with the building owner. Later, with an established track record, Time Energy raised about $20 million in two stock offerings. With a good idea in creative hands, money flowed to the idea, and Brown got Time Energy off to a rapid start. This is another example of an entrepreneur creating needed resources, here by an imaginative approach to financing.

When a few Americans became fascinated with small European automobiles after World War II and began to import them privately the idea caught on. Many manufacturers saw the potential of the American market and began shipping cars to the United States. Among the numerous British, French, Italian, and German manufacturers Volkswagen seems to have understood the American market best; it began immediately to build a dealer-service network. For lack of similar support most of the other entrants failed and withdrew from competition, leaving Volkswagen as the preeminent importer until the Japanese entered. The VW cars were good, but so were some of the others. Only Volkswagen had created the service-support resource necessary for survival.

The underlying argument is that business success requires a sound strategy and a part of that strategy is to obtain or create the necessary resources. Whether this means assembling, motivating, and training a superbly effective distribution team, as in the

---

[7] Robert H. Bork, Jr., "He Who Laughs Last," *Forbes*, July 15, 1984.

Frito-Lay case, or a novel means of obtaining financing, strategies are founded in part on the creation of needed resources.

Just as a colonial cabinetmaker often made specially shaped tools for each new type of furniture, business strategy often requires new tools for a specific purpose. Resources are among management's tools for reaching its goals. The art is to decide which resources can be created, and how to create them on a timetable and within a budget.

SUMMARY: STRATEGY, POLICY, AND THE BUSINESS FIRM

Strategies are basic approaches a management selects for designing the action to solve a problem or accomplish a goal. Policy constitutes the rules management makes for itself to guide the operation of the business. These rules can be the result of specific decisions, for example, when a new direction is chosen, or can grow out of habitual operating patterns. Management has complete freedom to make these rules so long as no laws are broken;

The mission—a key and defining social role.

Economic means—yield social ends and profits.

Make up your own rules—but be good at it.

ABOVE ALL, LEARN HOW TO CREATE RESOURCES

Figure 1.2. Fundamentals

therefore the success of a business often depends on the creativity of its management in making up rules and creating resources to enhance the strategic and competitive position of the enterprise, as summarized in Figure 1.2.

The purpose of the three chapters in Part 1 of this book is to provide an overall picture of strategy, policy, and the business firm, to define the underlying flow from planning to strategy to action and the specific links from mission to goals to strategy illustrated in Figure 1.3. By building on the foundation provided in Chapter 1, Chapter 2 deals with the way in which habits become

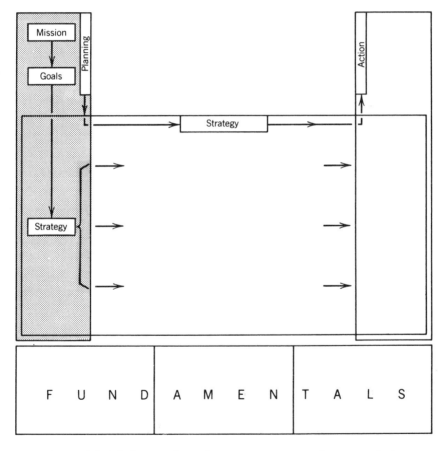

Figure 1.3. Mission, goals, and strategy as a part of strategy design.

policy and the formulation of strategy as the basis for both. Strategy, however, has different parameters at different levels and Chapter 2 also introduces the concept of primary strategy, which guides product, business, or enterprise development, and the need to design each of these three levels of primary strategy separately. Chapter 3 presents the components of enterprise strategy first because they govern the others, thus leaving the elements of product and business strategy to be discussed in Part 2.

═2

HABITS, POLICIES, AND STRATEGIES

Strategies and policies develop by spontaneous processes as a business operates. Both are normally improved by conscious assistance to their evolution. This chapter starts with the consideration of that process. It moves through mission and goals to strategic management and then to a more formal definition of the levels of strategy and the relationship between them.

HABITS AND POLICIES

An organization, like a person, develops habits that govern its actions. A firm decides to give each employee two weeks paid vacation after the first year. In another company the treasurer

Figure 2.1. Actions lead to policies.

conserves the firm's cash by telling his staff to "age" all invoices before paying them. These patterns of action quickly become habits. Operating habits soon become the policies by which an organization runs (Figure 2.1). They may develop as informally as a person's habits.

Employees occasionally become ill and companies sometimes arrange for paid sick leave on an individual basis. To control costs and to avoid helping one employee and not another it becomes necessary to define, publish, and enforce a sick-leave policy. Again, accepting small orders or creating special products for individual customers becomes a bad habit in some sales areas and raises costs; the need for cost control may lead to a policy to limit these orders. The larger the organization, the more likely the policies will be put in writing and issued officially.

CARRYING POLICY INTO ACTION

The purpose of a policy is to guide action. The span of possible policy problems, a large one, ranges from issues relating to equal opportunity and the proper handling of the people in the organization, to the central thrust of the business and the selection of appropriate areas and strategies for new ventures. In each case the payoff comes only at the point of management action—either action taken, or action avoided.

Action derives from strategy and policy only when the results are communicated. Line management must then act on the desired policies and enforce them. When a new policy is announced, experienced managers in some companies will wait for a clear indication that the company is serious about the change. Only when they see that the new policy has solid top-management support will they begin to put it into action.

STRATEGIC MANAGEMENT

Before it can be effective, strategy must be created, converted into policy, communicated, and made to work. In making it work, the integration of a well-conceived strategy with management of the ongoing business process is now being called **strategic management.**

Strategic management as a term came into general use as a result of conferences in 1973 and 1977 and the books that followed,[1] plus the ongoing work of Ansoff, Hofer, Schendel, and others. The original and continuing concept of management itself includes planning, or prevoyance in Fayol's terminology;[2] it therefore includes strategy formulation and execution. Some have attacked "strategic management" as redundant because the concept "management" already includes the concept "strategy" or "strategic" as a component.

Much actual management practice has not been effective in integrating strategy into operating routines; thus the extra emphasis carried by the designation "strategic management" is well justified. Also, recent studies of strategy and the strategy formulation process have led to new insights by which the integration of strategy into management as it was practiced by Fayol and other management pioneers can be enriched and increased in effectiveness.

The concept of strategic management places emphasis on resource creation and on an action output from the strategy and policy process. Strategy must be translated into policy and then into action to have meaning, and the proper action arises from a given set of strategies and policies as the result of effective strategic management.

[1]Based primarily on the 1973 conference: H. I. Ansoff, R. P. Declerc, and R. L. Hayes eds., *From Strategic Planning to Strategic Management* (New York: Wiley, 1976); based on the 1977 conference: Dan E. Schendel and Charles W. Hofer, *Strategic Management: A New View of Business Policy and Planning* (Boston: Little, Brown, 1979); continuing interest led to foundation of the Strategic Management Society and *Journal of Strategic Management;* see also H. Igor Ansoff, *Implanting Strategic Management* (Englewood Cliffs, N.J.: Prentice-Hall, 1984).

[2]Henri Fayol, *General and Industrial Management,* trans. Constance Storrs (London: Pitman, 1949); first published in French in 1916.

MISSION, GOALS AND STRATEGY

A business organization can make a profit only by a commercial transaction in which it sells goods or services for more than they cost to deliver; the difference is the profit. When a person or a business buys, the sale is accomplished by exchanging purchasing power—whether cash, check, or credit—for that good or service. The exchange takes place because the buyer finds the good or service more valuable than the purchasing power that must be surrendered. Thus the buyer is, in terms of his or her own personal value system, better off for having made the purchase.

The excess of value which causes the buyer to be better off means that society as a whole should be better off because the business is operating—it is fulfilling a beneficial social role. The survival of the business presupposes this role, which is its mission.

By performing its mission the business creates the opportunity to sell goods and services at a profit. If it does not perform well, too few will buy and the business will cease to exist. The profit incentive is crucial to business performance, but underlying the concept of the business must be a beneficial social role sufficient to create the profit opportunity.

Within the scope of the mission tangible targets are necessary; these are the goals. The mission is the basic social role and the goals are the specific targets within the framework of the role that management is working to achieve. Thus the mission of a brewer may be to supply the light lager beer needs of a region; as its goals management may strive to increase sales until the brewery is running at 90% of capacity and to raise profitability to the target level.

Some managers put goals in personal terms: "I want to reach $100 million in sales before I retire." If this retirement date is a number of years away, this goal could lead to a long-term plan for building the business. If this retirement date is close, the resulting actions could be short-term and not geared to future needs. When the major management goals are for near-term achievements, such as profitability for the current quarterly report, the future of the business may be neglected. Long-term goals often require investments that achievement of short-term goals will not allow;

therefore the reconciliation of long-term and short-term goals is an urgent and recurrent problem for any management group.

In working to achieve goals, it is necessary to have some sort of a plan of action, whether formal or informal. The core and directing element of a plan is the strategy, the basic approach to the problem; the flow is from mission to goals to strategy and action, as shown in Figure 2.2.

Strategy has been called the road map to the goals. In business it is the art or science of using available and newly created business resources with maximum effectiveness in moving toward the targets of the business. The execution of a strategy often involves competitive confrontations; therefore the analogy to a military battle plan or the competitive strategy of a game is apt. Lessons from game theory and battle strategy are often useful in certain business situations.

THREE LEVELS OF STRATEGY

To understand the strategy design process it is desirable to separate strategy into three levels: (1) the level dealing with the enterprise as a whole; (2) the level dealing with the operation and development of specific businesses; and (3) the level dealing with individual products and product strategies. These are the most important types of primary business strategy, as contrasted with support strategies.

Primary strategy is aimed at creating a pattern of action that will result in a specific accomplishment, whether for a firm, business unit, or product. Support strategy, which is more limited, deals only with the pattern of action by which a specific function, department, or other unit contributes to the accomplishment of a primary strategy. The primary strategies govern.

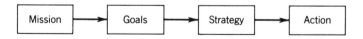

Figure 2.2. The mission as the starting point.

Occasionally it is necessary to deal with program strategy. This term is used for a group of related products within a product line: for example, Coca-Cola might consider the several light and diet Coke variations together under a program strategy that would coordinate the handling of all products using that brand name; program strategy might also be defined for a major cluster of activities in a service department or public agency. In either case program strategy is a potential intermediate level between the product and business strategy levels and can be accommodated easily when the need occurs.

The two basic types of strategy, primary and support, are summarized in Figure 2.3. Primary strategy varies by levels according to the scope of the business considerations that govern it. Support strategy varies by purpose according to the function or unit that strategy is designed to guide. Primary strategy guides the implementation of some portion of the business process of the enterprise, and support strategy guides a specific function or component of the business in support of the primary strategies.

The many organizational elements that may need to define a support strategy include all normal functions and components, and examples include research strategy, marketing strategy, department strategy, the night shift machine shop strategy, and

Types	Levels	Purpose
Primary strategy	Enterprise Business Product	To govern progress toward mission and goals
Support strategy	Department or other functional unit	As appropriate to support primary strategies

Figure 2.3. The types and levels of strategy.

the executive dining room staff strategy. They also include strategies for any unit that can have a plan, because any plan will have a chosen or implied strategy at its core.

Many strategies are named after the organizational unit or function they are designed to drive. An effective production strategy, for example, may be an essential component of a business strategy and will form the basis for planning the production unit and other units of the company whose activities synchronize with production.

PRIMARY STRATEGY

The three levels of primary strategy define the business potential that component and functional strategies work to optimize. Product strategy—or service strategy in the case of a service business—is designed for progress toward the product or service goals and drives the plan for the product. The limits of its achievement, whether due to the product or the strategy, set a limit on the potential that the component and functional strategies can achieve; that is, without good products and a good product strategy functional performance is limited, as is the performance of a business built on these functions.

Business strategy, the next higher level, is designed for progress toward the business goals and sets the limits of achievement of a business unit that may be made up of large numbers of products or services. It uses the product or service strategies as a base and integrates them into a whole whose potential may be greater or less than the sum of the individual product or service strategies, depending on the nature and effectiveness of the required integration. Poorly matched, the strategies for different products can cause them to interfere with each other's performance. Or, synergism can develop among good products because of the skill with which business strategy integrates them.

The highest of the primary strategy levels is that of the enterprise strategy, the key framework that controlls the general plan of accomplishment for the enterprise as a whole. It is discussed in more detail in Chapter 3. Enterprise strategy governs the program for moving toward overall goals and apportioning assets and capabilities, business strategy provides the core for the planning and action in a specific business area, and product strategy provides the same core for the planning and action programs for a specific product or service.

When this hierarchy of three levels of primary strategy is matched against the component or support strategies that relate to it, the linkages are those required by the logic of the situation; that is, a production or research strategy must be based on specific types of product; therefore it should support those product strategies as well as the strategy of the business of which the products are a part. The component strategy should also fit the requirements of the resource and other enterprise strategies that govern the products. Thus the component strategy, such as, in this case, a production or research strategy, will form the core of the action plan for the appropriate functional units after it is properly related to the requirements of these higher level strategies.

STRATEGY SUMMARY

By definition of the mission for each business and for the enterprise as a whole, and by selection of goals within the scope of the missions, management lays the groundwork for a clear-cut outline of strategy.

The three primary strategy levels (product, business, and enterprise) require both a bottom-up and a top-down approach. Because product and business performance is built on customer purchases in the face of competition, the business and the total enterprise must be built up on the basis of products or services successfully sold. From this point of view each product plan is an element that must aggregate into a business and into the total for the enterprise.

The top-down approach interacts with these product and business plans in two ways. In the first place, investments are usually required to achieve the full potential of a product or business. Therefore the attractiveness of each to top management must be sufficient to merit that investment. Further, a given enterprise sets out to operate within a pattern and establishes a corporate personality. Each operating unit contributes to that pattern and personality and when management wishes to reshape them some products and businesses are added and others are sold or withdrawn from the market.

Subordinate to the primary strategies are the functional and unit strategies as different organizational components define the requirements for their contribution to the accomplishment of these primary strategies. Program strategies represent an intermediate between product and business strategy levels used whenever a group of products, services, or other activities has characteristics that make coordination of their strategies and actions sufficiently desirable to justify the additional effort. The concept that unifies and directs these types and varieties of strategy is the fundamental flow from mission to goals to strategy and action, as illustrated in Figure 2.4.

It should be noted that in constructing Figure 2.4 and the other figures based on the planning and strategy to action sequence it was not intended to suggest that strategy design is other than a part of the planning process—only that, as the principal subject here, strategy and its components are expanded as the primary area of attention.

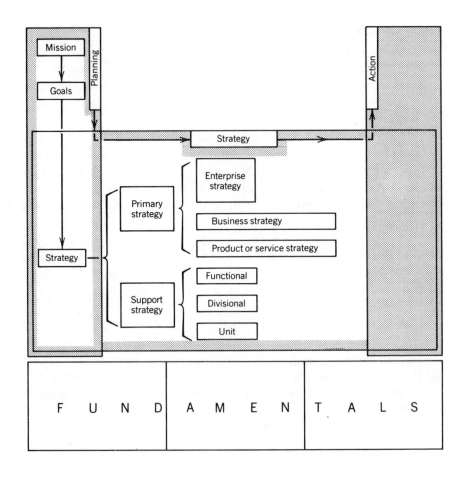

Figure 2.4. Action as the objective.

=3

THE GOVERNING STRATEGIES

All enterprises have strategies of their own, as differentiated from the strategies of the businesses they contain. This chapter is devoted to a discussion of these governing strategies. Ansoff[1] recognized the difference between the strategy for a specific business and the enterprise as a whole. This recognition was carried forward by Newman[2] and Steiner[3] in the concept of a firm's master strategy and as "developing a distinctive competence at the

---

[1]H. I. Ansoff, *Corporate Strategy* (New York: McGraw-Hill, 1965)

[2]William H. Newman, James P. Logan, and W. Harvey Hegarty, *Strategy, Policy, and Central Management,* 9th ed. (Cincinnati: South-Western, 1985).

[3]George A. Steiner, *Strategic Planning: What Every Manager Must Know* (New York: Free Press, 1979).

corporate level," by Berg.[4] It is important to make this clear-cut distinction between enterprise strategy, which governs and limits a firm's one or several businesses and the subordinate strategies within them.

Resources are created and applied within the realm of individual businesses, but the ability of a unit to undertake a specific business or product strategy is largely determined by the nature of the enterprise of which it is a part. Even in a one-product firm the nature of the resulting enterprise becomes a reinforcement to or a constraint on the strategies the business and product managers propose.

To understand strategy design, therefore, and the processes of creating and allocating resources, separate consideration of the enterprise, business, and product strategy levels is required, starting with enterprise strategy.

ENTERPRISE STRATEGY AND THE BUILDING BLOCKS

Enterprise strategy is assembled from components and is different in nature from the strategy for a specific product or business, because at the enterprise level the firm sells nothing and meets no customers; that activity is at the business and product levels. Enterprise strategy differs in quality and is more global. Instead of building and maintaining product or business positions and profits, it deals with decision elements, determining the sort of enterprise a firm wishes to be, and what the criteria should be for directing its energies.

The enterprise uses five building-block strategies to shape its own nature and five choice criteria in its resource decisions. The building blocks are (1) leadership, (2) opportunity, (3) people, (4) public, and (5) resource strategies, which are discussed first. The five choice criteria for individual projects are the (1) desirability, (2) managing, (3) belonging, (4) credibility, and (5) payoff strategies.

[4]Norman A. Berg, *General Management: An Analytical Approach* (Homewood, Ill.: Richard D. Irwin, 1984), pp. 147–149.

Leadership Strategy

An enterprise can be run in many ways; the current literature contrasts Japanese and American leadership prototypes. A management group can interact informally and across organizational levels or use formal structure and organizational protocol to govern its actions. It can organize with heavy staff support of all line activities or minimize staff in favor of developing less specialized and more autonomous line managers. No single way is right for all organizations or all situations; alternative approaches are almost always possible. The choice defines a leadership strategy; its selection will have a profound effect on the way in which the total organization will perform over time.

Opportunity Strategy

Any enterprise will assume a posture toward opportunity and innovation, a limiting condition that will influence operations. Opportunity is unpredictable in its occurrence. Some enterprises maintain a separate stock of resources in order to be prepared to move quickly toward a purchase, acquisition, or other sudden chance for advantage. Other firms keep opportunity in its place, taking no initiative until management is sure that the time is absolutely correct and usually forgoing unscheduled chances. Still others define the need for opportunity, arrange for the necessary resources, and then set out to create that opportunity if it does not occur spontaneously.

People Strategy

An enterprise will have a posture toward its people, both workers and managers, and a degree of commitment to them that will have profound consequences for the other aspects of its operation. Some corporations make a specific effort to keep salaries and fringe benefits above or below the levels established by other companies and make a major effort to help their employees to achieve meaningful and rewarding careers.

A firm like IBM will attempt to create a sense of employee

security and an implicit guarantee of lifetime employment. Other firms feel free to lay off and rehire workers with every shift in demand. Delta Air Lines, which has a longstanding no-layoff policy, performed surprisingly well during a bad period for airlines, compared with competitors who used heavy layoffs to cut costs. Some analysts attributed this good performance to the extra enthusiasm and spirit of Delta employees as a result in part of this no-layoff policy.

Public Strategy

An enterprise will need a strategy for its public role and for the image it hopes to project to each of its many segments of the public. As Mobil did after the oil embargo, it can decide to be aggressive in its opinions, or maintain a low profile. It can also attempt to build and promote a strong philanthropic image, as Norton does. It can court the favor of the stock market, the analysts, and its shareholders, as many large corporations do, or ignore them all and concentrate on business. By accident or design this strategy will be created and the other actions of the enterprise will be colored and conditioned by it.

Resource Strategy

Because of the nature of the business and its assets and because of management's attitude toward investment, debt, and sources of funding, some firms have money to spend and others do not. Hoffmann-La Roche long avoided debt and kept sufficient funds on hand for capital construction, acquisitions, and other current needs. Most businesses rely more on borrowed money but differ widely on the size of the debt burden they will consider carrying. Some firms borrow only with difficulty and by mortgaging their physical assets, and others develop skill at resource creation and an aura of success such that almost any need for funds can be accommodated.

Many corporations will sell common or preferred stock to raise additional capital from equity investment whenever market conditions are favorable. Some firms, however, particularly smaller ones, fear the dilution of present stock holdings by new issues and suffer delays in growth rather than sell equity.

Building an Enterprise

By its planned and unplanned choices in the five building-block areas management fixes many elements in the character and nature of the enterprise, even more than they are fixed by the nature of the businesses in which it participates. By the choice of its leadership strategy, its posture toward opportunity, its people strategy as revealed by its employment practices, its public strategy, and in the way it obtains the resources it needs, the enterprise sets boundaries that often determine the types of business in which it is likely to do well or badly.

ENTERPRISE CHOICE CRITERIA

Management decisions in the five building-block areas largely determine the basic nature of the enterprise, but the firm is created in actuality by a flow of decisions, as support is given to some proposals and denied to others. This is the area of enterprise choice strategy. Its decisions are based on standards of desirability, managing, belonging, credibility, and payoff.

Desirability Strategy

How worthwhile or how important is any single activity in the light of the mission and goals? How favorable and unfavorable are the personal and organizational dynamics of this opportunity? Major companies often enter a new field by acquiring a small company from which the business can be expanded, and often management will be willing to pay much more for the initial acquisition than it would have otherwise because of its desirability as a starting point for a major program.

Although each proposed activity should be able to stand on its own merits, overall considerations sometimes enter. All industries in all countries are not equally attractive for investment; for example, Abegglen[5] pictured the Japanese economy as shifting toward higher value-added industries and deemphasizing the others, with Japanese companies now encouraged to invest in chemical and other facilities in other Asian countries to provide sources of material formerly manufactured at home, to the point that even the Japanese steel industry has become relatively unattractive for further investment in Japan itself. A company may have a good opportunity even in a declining industry, but the overall set of economic and political currents that make a given industry in a given country seem likely to advance or decline casts a favorable or unfavorable light on the desirability of any specific project.

Managing Strategy

Manageability is a primary basis for management choice in almost every case in which investment in more than one business area is being considered. Some managements feel that they should limit themselves to one or two types of business, but others are casual about moving into any area in which the financial returns appear attractive.

During its early growth phase U.S. Industries made much of its desire to acquire any company in any business as long as it had good prospects for growth and profitability. Yet W. R. Grace, a successful company classified as a conglomerate by many analysts, divested businesses and rearranged into a chemical and consumer sales company in order to have a more identifiable and manageable business pattern. Avon Products long concentrated its energies on continuing successful growth in the direct sales area and then began to broaden into other marketing. William Wrigley, Jr., the leading chewing gum company, has continued to concentrate its energies in that one product area. These examples represent managing strategies pursued by different firms. Management's choice among different investment opportunities is heavily conditioned by its own feelings for the span over which its manage-

---

[5]James C. Abegglen, *The Strategy of Japanese Business* (Cambridge, Mass.: Abt/Ballinger, 1984).

ment will be most effective. This is a key element in enterprise choice strategy.

Belonging Strategy

This element of choice strategy is closely related to manageability. It includes a judgment of the comfort of management with a proposed project, its fit with the rest of the enterprise, and the controllability of that activity within the organizational framework. Management should be able to manage each area in which it has put resources and it should feel comfortable about the process, lest discomfort lead to hesitation and mistakes. Several of the leading ethical drug manufacturers did not invest in research on birth control products because they did not believe they would feel comfortable marketing them; then after society accepted the oral contraceptives and made them respectable, some of these companies belatedly joined the product-development race.

Fit is the relationship of one business element or activity to the others around it. It can be a significant consideration because good fit helps with comfort and because sometimes there are worthwhile economies of scale when several similar activities can be carried out jointly better than any one of them alone.

Controllability represents the management's judgment as to how well a particular activity would fit into the management operating system and how well the present control system or one that has been modified would allow management to stay current with the events in that area.

Air Products & Chemical, a diversified industrial gas and chemical company, acquired Adkins-Phelps, a strong regional herbicide and pesticide distributor, as a first step in a major diversification into agricultural chemicals which was not carried further. The acquisition was a compatible one; Adkins-Phelps continued its profitable growth and related well to Air Products management.

As a seasonal business, Adkins-Phelps completed almost all of its annual sales in a six-week period, with correspondingly wide swings in inventory and cash requirements. Although Air Products had managed it adequately, the question was whether anyone at the corporate center really understood the Adkins-Phelps business well enough to detect anomalies or to react if it began to get into trouble. Management decided the risk was too great and that it should sell Adkins-Phelps and invest instead in more familiar areas.

Credibility Strategy

In any choice between alternative uses of resources the quality or credibility issue should be an important one. Regardless of how large or exciting the potential opportunity may be, is the specific plan being proposed a sound and workable one and can the specific manager or group carry out the plan to turn the invested resources into the expected returns? Unless the plan is sound and the chosen managers capable of making it work, the project should not be approved. Although most managements react intuitively against a weak plan in a familiar area, they do not always ask enough searching questions, particularly about operations in unfamiliar areas; therefore explicit treatment of this element of choice strategy is important.

Payoff Strategy

This element of choice strategy is included automatically in most financial systems, at least to some calculation of return on investment or discounted cash flow for the project. The actual dimensions of the choice are larger. Few projects are truly certain of achievement and the actual probability of success can be estimated only approximately at best. Management's investment decisions will be based on some composite of the projected returns and apparent risks. This judgment process should be made as open and uniform as practical to allow projects of equal attractiveness to be uniformly funded or rejected.

Choice Strategies

The flow of decisions based on the desirability, managing, belonging, credibility, and payoff strategies go a long way toward determining strategy at the enterprise level. They are based on simple questions: (1) Is this a good step in the development of our business? (2) Can we manage this project or business? Is it good use of our talent to try? (3) Will we be comfortable operating it? Will it fit with our other operations? Will be be able to control it? (4) Is this a sound plan presented by managers who can make it happen? (5) Are the potential rewards large enough to justify the risks?

The purpose of the choice strategies is to guide the continual process of analysis and decision among alternative projects and ventures. Although the building block strategies define the capabilities and shape the public perception of the enterprise, the reality is sustained by the product and business activities that make continued existence of the enterprise possible. The choice strategies are the key to this sustenance.

SUMMARY: ENTERPRISE STRATEGIES AND ACHIEVEMENT STRATEGIES

There are three levels of primary strategy. Enterprise building block and choice strategies, summarized in Figure 3.1, are at the highest level; business and product strategies are subordinate. Enterprise strategies largely determine the nature and capabilities of the firm as a whole. The product and business strategies drive the action in the market place, and the functional and unit strategies make possible the accomplishment of the primary strategies they support.

Each business is driven by a mission and a set of goals; therefore business and product strategies are goal-oriented achievement strategies. Enterprise strategy is less consciously designed, sometimes developing spontaneously or as an extension of the style and capabilities of the executive group. Therefore it is less results-oriented and can often be achievement-limiting in its consequences. Market action builds from product or service strategies assembled from the appropriate elements. These strategies become part of an achievement-oriented business strategy, but both are governed by enterprise strategies that could be based on

Building Block Strategy, determines the type of enterprise that management will build.

LEADERSHIP STRATEGY. The manner and degree of formality or informality with which the management group chooses to work amongst itself and with the organization as a whole.

OPPORTUNITY STRATEGY. The aggressiveness or passiveness of the opportunity search and the way in which detected opportunities are evaluated and developed.

PEOPLE STRATEGY. The kind of employee community and the nature of the teamwork and of the long- or short-term relationships that the organization builds and maintains.

PUBLIC STRATEGY. The degree of impact of enterprise actions on the public, the extent to which this is open and visible, and the way in which this role is managed.

RESOURCE STRATEGY. The money-spending and money-obtaining policy and the way in which it interrelates with the other strategies.

Choice Strategy is the basis for allocating resources, project by project.

DESIRABILITY. The degree to which a specific project is a good thing in the light of what the enterprise and its managers are and are trying to become.

MANAGING. How diverse or how homogeneous the enterprise should be, how many types of management challenge should be compounded, and how complex the overall management task should be permitted to become.

BELONGING. The degree to which a given product or business will mesh into the fabric of the enterprise.

CREDIBILITY. For each request for management approval the quality of the underlying plan and the ability of the managers proposing to make it work.

PAYOFF. The acceptability of the projected payoffs and the likelihood that they will be achieved.

Figure 3.1. Components of enterprise strategy

personal executive preferences to the point that they can make otherwise viable product and business strategies impossible to accomplish.

As governing strategies, the five building blocks and five choice strategies are as important as if they really were 10 commandments written on two tablets of stone (Figure 3.2).

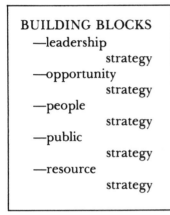
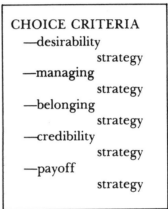

BUILDING BLOCKS
—leadership
      strategy
—opportunity
      strategy
—people
      strategy
—public
      strategy
—resource
      strategy

CHOICE CRITERIA
—desirability
      strategy
—managing
      strategy
—belonging
      strategy
—credibility
      strategy
—payoff
      strategy

Ten commandments for your

organization—written by

accident or written by design?

Figure 3.2. Two tablets of stone

This chapter completes Part 1, which outlined the planning and strategy to action process and presented the three levels of primary strategy and discussed the first; the elements of product and business strategy are *discussed in Part 2. Enterprise strategies govern the overall function of the organization, including the choice of product and business strategy, and should be consistent with and supportive of the mission and goals of each business unit; but because of the casual development of enterprise strategy in some organizations inconsistencies occur. The review and possible modification of enterprise strategies are among the topics treated in Part 4.*

PART 2

Foundations for Strategy

=4

THE PRODUCT AS THE
BASIS FOR A STRATEGY

The first three chapters have presented an overview of the strategy/policy process. After defining mission, goals, and strategy the three levels of strategy were presented, plus the components of enterprise strategy, and the links required from strategy to policy to action to give strategy practical meaning.

No strategy will stand alone. It needs careful grounding in fundamentals. The purpose of Part 2 is to describe some of its foundations. Each of the next three chapters summarizes an area in which any strategy should be firmly grounded if it is to be successful (Figure 4.1). These areas are (1) the nature of the product or service, (2) the nature and structure of its markets, and (3) the characteristics of the business that offers the product. This chapter explores the nature of the product or service by starting

39

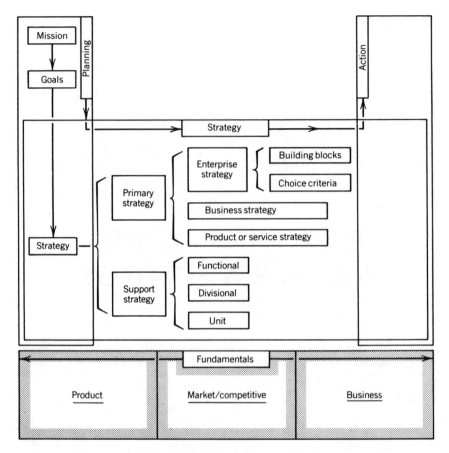

Figure 4.1. Foundations for strategy.

with the elements of its strategy, the degree of its differentiation, its life cycle, and its possible sources of profit in the market place.

ELEMENTS OF PRODUCT AND BUSINESS STRATEGY

Some strategies succeed and others fail. These successes and failures are attributable to a variety of factors, but failures often result from incompatible choices of components from which these strategies are constructed. Product and business strategy are built up, piece by piece, from a series of elements:[1] (1) the deliverable(s), (2) resources, (3) leverages, (4) focus, (5) positions, (6) display, and (7) cash flow.

Deliverable(s)

Product and business strategy aims ultimately at the generation of revenues by the sale of products or services. For this result to be achieved the business must have something to sell: a deliverable that must meet a customer need in the opinion of that customer; it serves as a satisfier of that need. A given deliverable may be positioned and promoted in a wide variety of ways, but at the end of the sales process it must transfer to the customer and fulfill a reasonable portion of that customer's expectations, or no sustainable commercial activity will result:

Resources

Resources are the available array of assets relevant to a specific strategy. Money is included because it is used to obtain other resources but it is not directly productive. Some resources are used up, as money is spent, and others such as a reputation for quality are created by a strategy and increased in value by its success.

Leverages

Leverages, which are the factors that persuade a customer to buy a specific product or service, may range from tangible elements such as price and product superiority to product image and the symbolism of ownership and use. Researchers suggested a few years ago that a man might buy a powerful convertible as a substitute for a mistress, and automobile advertising was keyed subtly to evoke this image as a product leverage.

With this and all other leverages, the operative truth is what the customer believes because these beliefs lead to the purchase. The art of using leverages as a part of a business strategy is the art of

---

[1]George C. Sawyer, "Elements of Strategy," *Managerial Planning,* May/June 1981, pp. 3–5,9.

inducing the customer to consider a given product or service as a desirable or essential purchase. A sales executive once explained leverages as the way to pry the customer's wallet open—a crude image, but one that conveys the importance of leverages clearly.

Focus

Focus is the desired relationship between seller and customer. In many retail product lines that relationship is entirely impersonal; for example, in the case of cosmetics that are sold in a variety store. Some manufacturers want a closer connection with customers and use beauty consultants in department stores to give assistance in choice and use of the cosmetic products in the line. Still others sell cosmetics to stylists who perform at least part of the product application—selling a beauty service as well—and give careful and repeated guidance on how the products are to be used.

All three approaches succeed. The products sold impersonally in the variety store must be the simplest and most foolproof. With personal demonstration and application can come increasingly complex products, but the price must be higher because the personal element in the product delivery system is expensive.

The importance of the focus component of strategy is that management define the relationship with the customers it intends, and learn the support costs and product-line requirements this relationship requires, the prospects for profit after paying these costs, and the manner in which that competitive product lines and support systems fit into the market place. Thus a manufacturer would probably not attempt to develop a personal relationship with variety-store cosmetic customers because the cost of the necessary beauty consultants would be hard to support, considering the relatively low-priced product lines these stores carry.

Positions

Positions are the franchises, the images, the production or materials cost advantages, the reputation, and other factors that can build up in the market place or inside the firm as a result of a successful business or product and make that success easier to sustain in the future. Coca-Cola created a valuable market image and brand franchise bringing repeat sales. In a commodity market however, a commanding cost position can follow from the economies of scale attained by achieving a dominant market share.

In another type of dominance IBM established a position in computers by the extent of its sales success, and new professionals entering the field need training on its equipment more than any other; the fact óf their having this training makes their subsequent purchase of IBM equipment more natural than that of its competitors. Thus there is a tendency for the breadth of IBM equipment use to give it a position as an industry standard that can perpetuate itself.

Because they are such a large factor in maintaining the success of a company or product, an important part of a strategy is to use the thrust of present efforts to build the strongest and most durable positions possible. This requires an understanding of the nature, strength, and value of the various types and how they may be built. If current sales also develop long-term positions, this can bring a significant increase in the return from that strategy.

Display

Display is the related group of actions necessary to cause customers to adopt whatever relationship with a specific product or service is required to make a purchase decision. As necessary, they can learn about the product, see it demonstrated, handle it or try it, and gain sufficient familiarity with it to buy it. Sometimes display involves establishing a distribution network to make the product widely available in showrooms or on counters. Or display may only require the type of promotion that will make the potential customers aware of the product. Display activities often overlap with efforts aimed at establishing a specific focus or with advertising of leverages intended to cause the customer to buy.

Cash Flow

Cash flow is a key element of strategy because cash is a resource regulator. Businesses pass through stages of growth, some of which are typified by cash requirements and others by cash return. Cash flow should be predicted in planning; deviation from cash-flow projections is sometimes the most sensitive indication of the true progress of a plan and its strategy. Cash flow must be managed especially carefully during the investment phase when a shortage of cash is chronic. Later, as the business begins to generate more cash than is currently needed, the return on the investment that represents true long-term profit begins.

Although profits are the overall measure of success, the rate at which cash must flow into a new and growing business is a critical factor, and larger-than-expected requirements can be a danger signal. Bankruptcy occurs when a growing company allows its sales to increase too fast in relation to its cash resources and cannot pay its bills. Then if a business does not begin to generate cash after it has become well established in the market place, the initial investment may never be recovered.

Design of the Product Line

A key consideration in the design of a business strategy is the nature of the line of products or services that will be offered. One extreme is to include every product that customers or market channels could possibly require. Companies build up thick catalogs this way, but although this method will satisfy a wide range of customer needs the business will then have a large inventory of low-volume products to handle. This raises handling and distribution costs and customers find that the sales representatives cannot learn enough about all of the products to explain their functions.

The other extreme, to handle a single product or service, is often a poor choice unless it sells in extremely large volume. Handling only one item is often expensive for the vendor and may serve the customer less well when there is a need to buy related or compatible products.

Most businesses develop a compromise based on a grouping of products or services for several but not all requirements of its customer group or market channel. The nature and viability of that compromise is a key part of the business strategy.

Product Strategy and Business Strategy

In building up a product strategy, the object is always to combine those elements that will yield the best possible results, given the nature of the product and the available resources. Similarly, a business strategy will be designed to realize the maximum potential from the available or obtainable products and resources; under the best conditions this will amount to more than the sum of the individual product potentials, but it could be less if the products do not fit well together. Therefore business strategy includes the nature and design of the line of products or services as one of these considerations (Figure 4.2) as well as a determination that the proposed product strategies are well designed.

By understanding the availability and extent of the resources and the strength and value of the potential leverages and by defining a strategy that focuses them on the customer and displays the product or service effectively, the business or product should achieve profitable current performance in minimum time and also construct positions that make this success easier to maintain in the future.

Elements of Strategy

A product or business strategy is derived from the elements profiled above in an iterative, interactive process. This process usually starts with a specific product or service or with its concept. To sell that product or service leverages must be found or created. Their nature and power will vary with the focus that is chosen, the nature and strength of the positions that exist, and the most feasible alternatives for display. Often a slight redefinition of the deliverable will make it fit better with a given focus and positions and create stronger leverages. Underlying all of this is a need for resources. The balancing of these elements will result in projections of cash flow that will suggest the degree to which the projected strategy meets criteria and goals set by management at the enterprise level; see Figure 4.3.

DELIVERABLE(S). The product or service (or the catalog of related products or services) for which the strategy is designed and which, in a cost-effective manner, must meet a customer's needs in the opinion of that customer; that is, the deliverable must be an effective satisfier of those needs.

RESOURCES. The necessary combination of technology, equipment, time, talent, money, and position required to implement a strategy successfully.

FOCUS. The defined relationship with the customers and the market place on which a strategy is based.

LEVERAGES. The specific incentive to buy a given product or service, as perceived by the buyer; the reasons why the customer sees the deliverable product or service as a satisfier of his or her specific requirements.

POSITION. Any consequence of past operations that can become a resource providing leverages for strategies. Valuable positions include those based on brand names and other market success, unusually effective production, service, distribution, or selling organizations, raw material costs or control, superior or protected processes and technology, cost advantages, unusual management or organizational competence, and strong ties to customer need and habit patterns.

DISPLAY. The arrangements necessary to allow potential customers to become sufficiently familiar with a product or service and how and where to buy it. Because it can bring additional interaction with the customer, display is often coordinated with focus and with advertising of the leverages.

CASH FLOW. A process measure and control element to predict and track the action pattern of a strategy and to gauge its vulnerability to sudden failure or success.

PRODUCT LINE (business strategy only). Choice of the line of products or services that will provide the best practicable development of the potential of the business.

Figure 4.2. Elements of product and business strategy.

Enterprise Strategy	Business Strategy	Product Strategy
Building Blocks	Deliverable(s)	Deliverable(s)
Leadership strategy		
Opportunity strategy	Resources	
		Resources
People strategy	Leverages	
Public strategy		
		Leverages
Resource strategy	Focus	
	Positions	Focus
Choice Criteria		
Desirability strategy	Display	
Managing strategy		Positions
Belonging strategy	Cash flow	
Credibility strategy		Display
	Product line	
Payoff strategy		
		Cash flow

Figure 4.3. The three levels of primary strategy.

DIFFERENTIATING THE PRODUCT

Products vary in their individuality from generic grocery offerings, which position themselves as completely standard and faceless, to famous gemstones that would be recognized immediately by jewelers all over the world. Products can be found at all points between these two extremes, but a classification into four principal stages serves to highlight the shift in product characteristics and guide the product planning process. These four stages of differentiation are (1) unique products, (2) strong specialties, (3) weak specialties, and (4) commodities (Figure 4.4).

Unique product   A product for which there is no substitute at any price in the opinion of the buyer.

Strong specialty   A product whose substitutes are sufficiently inferior that the buyer will willingly pay a premium price.

Weak specialty   A product sufficiently better than its substitutes that the buyer will always select it if price and other considerations are equal.

Commodity   A product normally bought from the seller with the best price or delivery among those able to meet the product specifications.

Figure 4.4.   Differentiating the product or service.

Unique Products

Unique products are those for which there is no substitute. Whether a substitute exists is a matter of customer opinion, and customers will vary in those opinions. One person looking for a painting will accept anything attractive within a certain price range, but another may insist on an English scene, and a third on a particular landscape by Turner. With the increasing specificity of the request, the range of choice is narrowed toward a unique product. Most purchasers will accept something else at some extreme of price differentiation, thus validating the generalization that every product has a substitute. In some cases, however, the price differentiation may be extremely large; for example, when an art collector bids a record auction price to obtain a particular painting.

When Loctite first offered its line of adhesives as a replacement for metal lock washers, comparable adhesives were not available commercially from other sources. A metal washer could still be used for most applications, but the properties of the adhesive made possible some assemblies in which a metal washer could not be used. For these specific uses the Loctite adhesive was a unique product whose only substitute was a less desirable assembly.

Strong Specialties

Strong specialties are products whose substitutes are so inferior that they bring a premium price. The Loctite adhesive was originally sold at a price about the same as the cost of the metal lock washer it replaced, but as its properties were recognized, users developed a strong preference for it, and used it even when it did not replace a metal washer, paying more to get a better result. This is the normal situation created by a strong specialty product. Almost every product has obvious substitutes, but the performance of strong specialty products is so superior to that of the alternatives that the purchaser will willingly pay the difference.

The marketer needs to be aware of the price limits of this preference because significant volume may otherwise be lost to admittedly inferior substitutes. Valium, a tranquilizer with strong specialty-product characteristics, was considered a unique product by some doctors because of the superior results achieved in the treatment of patients. At one point the State of California made a major issue over its cost and insisted that California doctors use phenothiazine tranquilizers instead for public assistance patients. The phenothiazines were an inferior treatment for some conditions, but the price of Valium was farther above the price of phenothiazines than the State felt that its advantages justified and insisted on the less effective medication. This is an example of the loss of market by a strong specialty product because one customer felt that the price premium was too great.

Weak Specialties

Weak specialties are products whose properties are good enough always to be chosen when price and all other things are equal; that is, a weak specialty is a better product whose degree of superiority is too small to justify a price premium. A weak specialty can be used to gain a market share as long as its price is the same as that of its competitors.

Many businesses with custom formulas, special blends, or other special-for-the-customer inducements are attempting to create weak specialty positions. They usually incur extra costs in customizing and must recover them by increased sales if they cannot raise the price. Technical service support for a mature product line can also help to give it weak specialty characteristics for customers who buy it, at least in part, to get access to the service.

Sometimes these strategies succeed. Hoffmann-La Roche strengthened its sales position in bulk vitamins with a series of special blends and formulations with weak specialty product appeal; one example would be the family of products designed for direct compression into tablets, introduced to simplify that type of processing for the purchaser.

Sometimes these strategies fail when extra costs cut margins and extra sales fail to materialize either because the special properties lacked sufficient appeal or because competitors created alternative weak specialties equally attractive to the buyer. A group of competitors can sometimes find themselves all offering extra product features or technical service support without gaining any competitive advantage.

Commodities

Commodities are products that are available from many manufacturers and are sufficiently standardized to be bought by choosing the vendor with the best price and delivery among those who can meet the product specifications. Many metals, grains, and chemicals are commodities, and skillful purchasers often attempt to convert specialties into commodities by establishing a clear set of specifications and inducing competitive bids.

PRODUCT LIFE CYCLES

Products have life cycles. New products become old and may be replaced by still newer products. The markets for them expand, contract, or change in other ways as the demand is affected by economic and social variables.

Product life cycles are of many kinds; Figures 4.5 and 4.6 illustrate two of the extremes. Figure 4.5 shows a life cycle typical of a capital goods item with a fixed total market or of a consumer product that will be replaced by a better one or a newer fashion. The item is brought to market as an innovation, experiences a period of evaluation and testing, wins market acceptance, and begins to sell rapidly. As its potential market becomes saturated, sales first peak and then fall to a replacement level, which may be too low for the product to remain. When a product is replaced by a better product the expansion of the market is cut off and sales fall.

Figure 4.6 represents a life cycle that starts in the same way but differs in that the product finds a permanent place in the market. As it matures, the sales shift from a growth curve to some other curve governed by variables affecting demand. This life cycle might be typical of a commodity like table salt, polyethylene, or vitamin C or of a consumer product like Listerine or Jell-O which wins and holds a market franchise over a long period of time.

These two life cycles are defined in simple terms and many intermediate forms exist, as well as subtleties which include the effects of changes in promotional support or modifications of the product. These simple cycles, however, provide the basis for suggesting that the optimum strategy for any particular business is related to the sort of products and product life cycles or services and service life cycles on which that business is based and to anything that may extend these life cycles.

A business based on sale of short-life-cycle goods or services determines its size and growth characteristics largely by the size and effectiveness of the development effort. Examples would be a business based on short-lived capital products such as new instruments or on one-time service projects such as the construction of a plant or the successful completion of an R&D project. The need in a short-lived-product business is to bring in new products or projects faster than the old ones are completed or fade away.

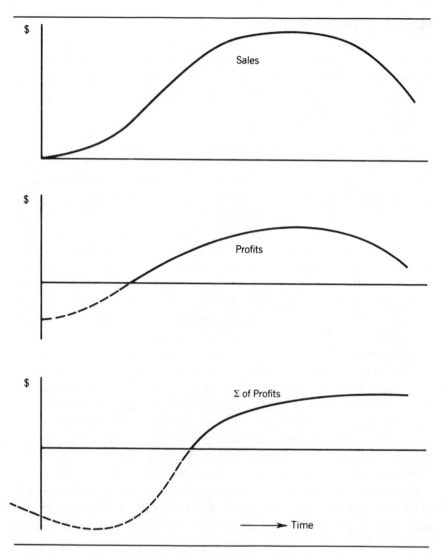

Figure 4.5. A short life-cycle product.

A business with long-lived products is different, for as it grows a larger and larger fraction of sales will be based on mature products in the later phases of their development. Management may become increasingly preoccupied with maintaining acceptable profit margins and therefore relatively less interested in new products.

In Figure 4.5 and 4.6 the profit curves show initial losses and a

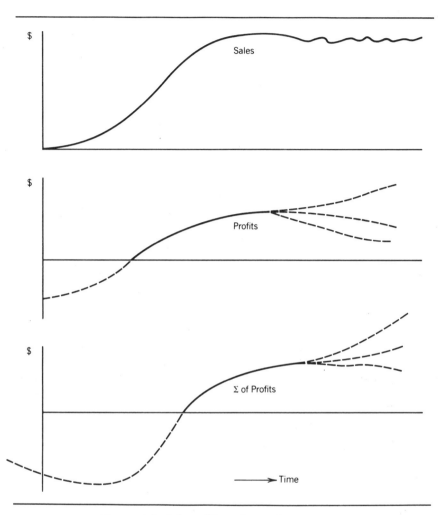

Figure 4.6. A long life-cycle product.

breakthrough into profitability at some point early in the rapid growth of sales. The curve for the summation of profits reflects the premarket costs and after-launch losses as investments, with start of repayment as the product becomes profitable, break even as the product approaches maturity, and finally a return on the investment.

The short-product-life business must be one of high innovation in that it must develop new products or sell new projects at least as fast as the old ones disappear if it wishes to exist over the long term. This product or project development is normally a significant expense, and an important fraction of the form's resources tends to be devoted to this activity.

Although the products or projects that result must be profitable on a current basis, it is equally important, on the average, that the profits exceed the initial investment. A frequent difficulty is the failure of a series of individually profitable projects or products to earn enough to repay the development costs fully. Consequently the firm consumes an element of its capital as each new activity moves through its life cycle and fades away.

The business with long-life-cycle products faces different challenges and problems. Initially each product passes through the same stages of development. Then, as it matures, it assumes different profit and market characteristics and the product strategy should change to reflect the changing basis of its competitive strengths.

SOURCES OF PROFIT FROM A PRODUCT OR SERVICE

Profit has many possible sources; it is important in the design of a strategy to understand those on which it depends. In his *Theory of Economic Development*[2] Schumpeter argued that the only true profit results from innovation. He emphasized the importance of the innovation process and the economic and public benefits of its high early rewards; but others are attracted by these profits, enter, and compete the profits away. When Schumpeter was asked to explain the money earned and reported as profit under other circumstances, he suggested that this often included interest, rent, and other types of earnings.

A broker or trader performs a service by making a certain type of transaction possible. This is the basis for a trading profit or fee. A wholesaler who buys in bulk and resells in smaller quantities earns a profit from this service. A retail merchant or industrial distributor performs a service by financing, distributing, and

[2]Joseph Schumpeter, *Theory of Economic Development* (New York: Oxford University Press, 1961).

promoting merchandise so that it can be located and purchased by the final consumer. For this service the merchant is entitled to be paid, and payment must compensate for the cost of the capital invested plus a proper allowance for risks in the transaction and a fee for the distribution service. Another type of profit would be the return to speculation or gambling, as in the commodity markets, in which the essential element is skill or luck in playing against risk or uncertainty.

When a high apparent profit level continues over a long time the nature of the money stream often changes. If established initially as the return to innovation this is a profit that will dwindle with time. For the same level of earnings to continue, other factors must begin to control. These factors are those that describe an advantage in cost or access to customers, justify a fee for a service, or represent barriers that prevent the entry of competition.

The return that they may properly earn is not an innovator's profit but often a form of rent. Rent was first defined based on the return to the owner for the poorest land whose income would cover the direct cost of production. This land would be farmed but would earn no rent. On richer land the production costs would be essentially the same but the yields would be higher, and the extra revenue from the larger harvest would be the amount of rent that the owner could obtain for the opportunity of farming his rich land.

The relevance of these distinctions to business and product strategy is that the money streams reported as profits in most businesses include other types of income, as illustrated in Figure 4.7. In economic terms these reported profits are a mixture of true profits from innovation, fees for making a market and for distribution services, interest on the capital employed, and rents based on entry barriers and advantageous positions in the marketplace.

Although stockholders generally do not care what brings in the money, the management of products and businesses generating different types of income requires different strategies. When a product comes to market as an innovation and continues to show a return after the innovation has lost its newness, this occurs because the management of the product has caused, or at least permitted, this continuation on the basis of different sources of profit.

TRUE PROFIT

The *returns to innovation.*

FEES

For *distribution services.* Making merchandise conveniently available for purchase. Retailing of all sorts, mail-order outlets, industrial distributors, and supply houses.

For *manufacturing services.* Making or assembling products that would not otherwise be conveniently available.

For *trading services.* Bringing together interests of buyer and seller. Securities and real estate brokers, trading between countries.

For *breaking bulk.* Reselling lesser quantities not otherwise available. Odd lots of common stock, small bags of coal, or potting soil for plants.

For *use of capital.* A return on the investment required for the business pattern. Financing of retailer via trade credit from wholesaler, hospital supply inventory necessary to guarantee same-day delivery.

For *insurance.* Inventory and other business risks carried in the customer's interest. Spoilage and obsolescence of inventories, hedging of commodity and currency risks.

For *specialized services.* Customs processing, personal shopping, custom design.

Figure 4.7. Types of business profit (Where **profit** is the net return from a particular business activity after direct and allocated costs and taxes).

RENTS

Earned by *differential productivity of resources*, such as a superior cost position.

Based on *brand names*, reputation, customer habits, or other market franchise.

Due to *patents*, trade secrets, control of natural resources, or any other sort of monopoly position.

Due to *economies of scale* in purchasing, production, distribution, or marketing.

Figure 4.7. Continued.

ELEMENTS OF STRATEGY AND SOURCES OF PROFIT

Starting with leverages as the specifics that encourage purchase at a given price, one source is likely to be in the deliverable and based on the innovations that it represents or the positions that protect it. To the extent that the leverages leading to the sale are from innovation the profit is pure in the Schumpeterian sense. As other elements also emerge, other considerations enter.

General Foods has a valuable market franchise in the Jell-O product and trade name. No longer an innovation, this product is believed to return an attractive profit. This profit includes a fee for manufacturing and distribution services—in that General Foods makes the Jell-O product widely and conveniently available—but where generic pudding products intended to serve the same customer need are available at one price, Jell-O commands a somewhat higher price. The difference is a profit of another sort—rent, in the economic sense—as a price premium earned by the strength of the franchise for Jell-O which good marketing of a good product has established over the years. If because of higher volume General Foods' cost of goods is lower than that of their generic competitors, the difference represents a separate sort of rent earned by the production and distribution position and adds to the total reported as profit.

In managing a product such as Jell-O, the nature of the different sources of profit is a proper part of the framework of the product strategy. As these sources change with the evolution of the product life cycle, optimum product strategy will shift correspondingly.

When Librium was first marketed in 1963 it represented an important innovation, soon followed by the parallel but somewhat different innovation of Valium. These two products had utility as tranquilizers not possessed by predecessor products, and both appear to have a permanent place in tranquilizer therapy.

Both products are known to have been profitable for the company that brought them to market and the initial profits were clearly a return to innovation, but as they matured the continuing money flows were no longer innovator's profits.

Generic chlordiazepoxide, the Librium substance, has been available for several years at a fraction of the Librium price but has been slow to penetrate because of the strength of the Librium market franchise. Traditionally, the prescription drug market is willing to pay a high rent—again in the economic sense—to the holder of an established product franchise, in part because of a continuing concern over quality differences in generic products and more because the doctors who prescribe the product find it easier to practice medicine by keeping constant the drug, which is a small part of the treatment, and varying other factors in search of better health response from their patients.

Not all pharmaceutical companies appear to be sensitive to the inevitable shift of a new product profit base from innovation, from which Librium profits were initially derived, to rent based on accumulated positions and franchises plus a distribution fee, which have since become the basis for Librium profits. Failure to understand this shift could lead to errors in product management.

More dramatic is the consistent shortfall of the recurrent activist and public-sector attempts to establish generic prescription products as a means of cutting pharmaceutical company profits. This failure is due in part to a fundamental misunderstanding of the nature of the franchise upon which the use of the higher priced products depends. Had the drug companies and their opponents developed a clearer understanding of the source of the profits they have been quarreling over, several firms might have fared better competitively in the transition from managing innovative products to collecting rents and distribution fees. Also the generic prescription efforts might have gained market share more quickly.

The central point for product and business management is to identify the different sources of profit on which a given product or business depends and then to develop a strategy to make the best use of this potential by using leverages based on the positions that earn each sort of actual or potential profit.

When Xerox launched its major early leasing program it was choosing to sell a copy service on a per-copy basis rather than to sell copy machines. Although the consequence—making Xerox copies—was the same, the copy-service concept brought in another source of profit in addition to bypassing customer concern for financing machinery capital costs.

In its period of early growth American Hospital Supply removed a large part of the investment and inventory risk in hospital supplies from customer hospitals by guaranteeing quick delivery of a wide variety of items. The hospitals were relieved of the need to order until the products were actually required, thus allowing them to operate with little inventory. The distributor was paid for these services but was better able to manage inventories and inventory risks; consequently the continuing distribution pattern was both economically efficient and profitable.

In the same way, insurance companies make a good business out of underwriting risks that they can manage more economically than client companies, and commodity speculators by their speculations permit hedging of grain purchase prices, which allows producers to enter into contracts for future delivery of meat or processed foods that would otherwise be too hazardous.

The number of examples could be multiplied further but the underlying point is this: there are many sources of profit in commercial transactions and innovation is only one of them, even though it may be the richest, long-term. Good strategy often involves the use of several sources of profit, but this diversity can be managed effectively only if the different profit elements are recognized for their contribution to the positions and leverages on which the sales volume depends, and for what each source of profit has cost to develop, in order that the resulting cash flows may be compared on a return-on-investment basis.

SUMMARY: LINKING STRATEGY TO PRODUCT

Product differentiation of commodities into specialties favors higher prices, and Levitt has argued that a skillful marketer can differentiate anything.[3] However, the inherent nature of the deliverable in a specific case may make it easier or harder to make that product or service into a specialty, and the nature of the positions that provide the leverages determines whether rent may be possible; for example, from a superior commodity cost position or a patent blocking competition. Further, the stage in the product life cycle and other circumstances under which the specific product or service will be made available to the buyer will indicate whether a distribution fee, return on risk or inventory investment, or other special income source is a proper addition to the income stream that product or service is designed to generate. A well-conceived product strategy will integrate the choices among its elements with an appropriate degree of differentiation, after consideration of the potential sources of profit from that product and the best short- and long-term approaches to generating them.

The elements of product and business strategy are governed by the enterprise building-block and choice strategies discussed in Chapter 3. The three levels of primary strategy were summarized in Figure 4:3, and, as indicated in Figure 4.8, considerations of the basic product or service characteristics and life cycle characteristics, both reviewed in this chapter, are foundations for an effective linkage from planning to strategy to action, as illustrated in Figure 4.9.

[3]Theodore Levitt, "Marketing Success Through Differentiation—of Anything," *Harvard Business Review*, January–February 1980, pp. 83–91.

Building product or service strategy from its elements

Deliverable(s)   Focus   Cash Flow
Resources   Positions
Leverages   Display

Choosing the best degree of product differentiation

Unique product   Weak specialty
Strong specialty   Commodity

Adding up the sources of profit from a product

Innovation   Fees for distribution, trading, risks,
Rents*   use of capital.

BUILDING SOUND PRODUCT STRATEGY

Figure 4.8. Product or service characteristics as fundamentals.

*Note: Economists often distinguish between *rents* for use of real estate, and *quasi-rents* for use of other sorts of property. For simplicity both are considered as rents here.

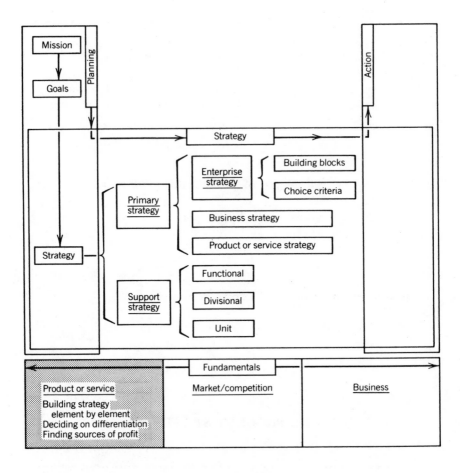

Figure 4.9. Product or service characteristics basic to strategy design.

≡5

THE MARKET AS THE BASIS
FOR A STRATEGY

Just as the nature of the product or service has dimensions that
condition the choice of an appropriate strategy, so has the nature
of the market in which it will be offered. This chapter considers the
key characteristics of the market and its life cycle, and the competition in that market.

THE NATURE OF THE MARKET

A market is the forum in which a product is exchanged for money
or other purchasing power—the forum in which the buyer and
seller or their agents meet, negotiate, and execute the exchange.
Markets vary widely in their characteristics—their organization,

63

information flows, geographic size and homogeneity, and the degree and nature of competition.

Organization

Some markets are rigidly and formally organized, as in the case of the New York Stock Exchange, on which only securities approved and listed in advance can be traded and on which the trading can be conducted only by the members of the exchange in accordance with a rigid pattern of trading rules. Most markets are less organized and less formal. In the markets for residential real estate and clerical employment, for example, the transaction process is more individual and less publicized but still a part of a broad competitive pattern. Yet other markets, for example, for idle steel mills or for the construction of a new electric power complex, differ so much according to the circumstances surrounding each buyer and seller that every transaction tends to be a unique event.

Availability of Market Information

Good market information is an important competitive tool and information availability varies widely from market to market. The New York Stock Exchange requires that the price and volume of every transaction be reported on an electronic display and the day's trading is summarized and published in newspapers all over the world. Although few markets build in such detailed reporting, specialized information services usually spring up, and one characteristic of a market is the extent and caliber of the information services available. Real estate prices and clerical wages are estimated by area surveys and audits of major consumer goods, drug, and other markets may be purchased. Information on special transactions, such as the sale price for a used manufacturing plant, may or may not be readily available; in this as in other specialized market areas accurate market information may be difficult to obtain.

Geographic Size and Homogeneity

The U.S. market for new Cadillacs seems homogeneous because General Motors makes one basic line of Cadillacs and sells them to distributors nationally at a reasonably uniform price. Yet the market is organized around a system of local dealerships, each with an advantage in its local area because it is closer to its customers and can serve their needs more conveniently than more remote agencies.

Many markets subdivide geographically. In the case of Cadillacs the subdivision is according to dealerships supported by groups of customers. Cement and sulfuric acid are heavy industrial products whose freight cost is high in relation to their market value. They tend to be manufactured regionally and shipped a minimum distance; competition is primarily at the territorial margin or against others manufacturing within economical shipping distance. The markets for fresh vegetables were once entirely local, but their shipping radius has been extended repeatedly by improvements in refrigeration and handling; California, Texas, and Florida growers now ship to the rest of the country.

Other factors determine market homogeneity, which is based on the degree to which most of the customers will buy the same product. The typewriter market was once relatively homogeneous because all offices were equipped with similar typewriters. Then development of portables opened up different home and college markets, electrics brought higher performance office applications, and now the evolution of word processing has further fragmented the market by supplying a wide variety of configurations that can link a typewriter or printer to a large or small computer.

In this case the different classes of customer always had different needs, but the market did not recognize these differences and some requirements went unsatisfied. The actual market was relatively homogeneous until a range of machines that performed more of the potential functions was developed and made available; the market expanded as a consequence. Now analysts predict narrowing, as computer/word processing applications evolve into a pattern that serves the present range of customer applications with a smaller number of printer/typewriters than at present.

In many markets the lack of homogeneity of customer needs is extreme. One manufacturer of bulk vitamins found it necessary to create separate sales and technical service forces for food-industry and animal-feed marketing of the same products in order to compete effectively for the business of customer companies with different and specialized needs based on the same vitamins.

Market Boundaries

The important market characteristics in designing business strategy and policy are those that determine how the market should be approached, beginning with size, boundaries, patents and other competitive barriers, and the nature and extent of present and predictable competition. It is important to examine these market characteristics to see how susceptible they may be to change as new products are developed and marketed—as the typewriter market changed and grew under the impact of successive innovations—and to judge how likely the necessary innovations may be and their most probable source.

MARKET EVOLUTION AND LIFE CYCLES

A market comes into being when an area of customer need is discovered and matched with goods and services with the potential for satisfying that need. Other sellers join the activity and compete for buyer interest. Other buyers discover the market and come to make purchases.

Changes as the Market Grows

The nature of the market can be changed, as the development of word processing expanded and changed the needs formerly served by typewriters. Boundaries of a market can change, for example, when U.S. drug and chemical companies accepted the idea of buying from other countries, competition in certain specialty chemical markets became international for the first time. The nature of the demand can change as customer industries pass through periods of prosperity and retrenchment, and the nature of the competition can change; for example, when oil producers entered petrochemical manufacturing and marketing in large numbers.

A market may develop when a major customer need appears; for example, the entry of Sears into retail markets outside the United States required an aggressive purchasing program to obtain local supplies of the necessary goods. Sears assisted a number of local firms in entering specific lines of manufacture. Thus the national capability to produce certain consumer goods was greatly increased and markets other than those of the Sears buyers were eventually supplied.

A market may be established by successful commercialization of a discovery; when the potential for making office calculators smaller and lower in cost was discovered, an aggressive, competitive new electronic calculator market resulted. A market may come into being as a result of new rules and regulations; environmental legislation created opportunities for laboratories to perform required animal and chemical testing for the market participants. It also created opportunities for specialized disposal firms to treat difficult wastes for waste-producing firms.

Evolution Through the Market Life Cycle

Typically, a newly created market is disorderly. The participants have not yet learned to work together smoothly, the pace of innovation leads to changing and imperfect production processes, and the new market attracts new entrants, each at a different state of readiness and with a different competitive effectiveness.

As a market becomes less new, the relationship established between buyers and sellers becomes more orderly. As the market grows, the sellers often overexpand. A shakeout is common, as more successful firms outdistance others and the number of competitors begins to drop. During a period of rapid overall growth the personal computer market went through a shakeout that eliminated Osborne among others.

Typically the rate of innovation in a market is highest at the beginning, declining later. Competitive barriers that limit entry to a new market are often short-term only. Know-how and trade secrets diffuse across the industry, patents are bypassed or expire, and the special advantages of one firm become smaller. The market is said to mature, as the competitive offerings become less differentiated, price competition sharpens, margins shrink, and demand becomes more cyclical. Perhaps the market will move on into a period of decline, as the growth of the auto industry caused the carriage and buggy-whip markets to decline.

Changing the Product and Market Life Cycle

The concept of different stages of a market life cycle is useful in the strategy formulation process. The caution, and the problem in strategy design, is that the structure and stage of development of a market is the consequence of the forces bearing on it in terms of innovation, competition, and consumer need. Any good strategy will be effective because it strengthens the position of the company that applies it. This has the potential for changing the situation in the market to a degree proportional to the effectiveness of that strategy.

Those who were around Elmer Bobst at the time tell of the acquisition of the Lambert Pharmacal Company to form today's Warner-Lambert, which Bobst long headed. Lambert had one important but obviously mature product—Listerine. When Bobst agreed to acquire Lambert for a price that stunned his subordinates, the Lambert family was happy; they had sold at a good price before the inevitable decline.

Bobst had a different view and began to promote Listerine as it had never been promoted before. Sales and profits skyrocketed, more than validating the purchase price. By an aggressive change in marketing strategy Bobst had rejuvenated an apparently mature product into a new growth phase, also revitalizing and expanding the mouthwash market in which it competed.

The point is that the useful, necessary classification of markets and life cycles before a strategy is defined is only tentative; all of these things can be changed. Changes as dramatic as Bobst's success with Listerine are uncommon but not unparalleled. Because innovation and profit margins are low in a mature market does not mean that either *must* stay low; a product with sufficient leverages and a well-chosen focus can break open a static market situation, bring new sales and profits, and permit the building of enduring positions, as the Warner-Lambert Listerine position still endures in today's market.

Market Structure

After a market becomes established, it tends to divide into the hands of a number of competitors with widely different market shares. Over time the number of competitors tends to shrink. Many analysts have studied this evolution of market structure.

One interesting approach to an analysis of market structure was Reith's at Du Pont. His Generalized Distribution Rule,[1] based on a statistical analysis developed by Kendall,[2] was intended to describe the equilibrium competitive balance between competitors in any market, given the number of competitors. Kendall's analysis is based on the size distribution of random numbers; in effect, Reith was treating markets as if the distribution of ability, innovation, resources, and therefore market success among competitors were a result of random processes. In the auto industry the Rule predicted that the largest of four competitors should have a 52% market share, General Motors' exact share of a U.S. auto market in the 1960s effectively divided among four companies. The remarkable fit Reith found between actual versus theoretical structure of the auto industry in the 1960s and in several other industries suggests that a random process could often be used for a first approximation of industry division between competitive firms.

This allows the construction of a useful model of the market and industry evolution process. In the early days of an industry, if a relatively large number of firms have market shares randomly distributed as to size—but totaling 100%, of course—as the industry then has good and bad years, the effects will be uneven. Typically, the larger firms have greater ability to withstand adversity, more margin to survive blunders, and intrinsically better profits because of scale economies at various stages in the development/production/distribution process. As an industry

---

[1] John E. Reith, "Generalized Distribution Rule," unpublished manuscript, Du Pont Textile Fibers Department, Wilmington, Del., April, 1967.

[2] M. G. Kendall, "Ranks and Measures," *Biometrika*, Vol. 49, pp. 133–139 (1964).

operates, therefore, the normal fluctuations jeopardize the small firms more, and occasionally one falls by the wayside, as Osborne Computer did.

New entrants are possible, but typically as a market evolves toward maturity it becomes more difficult for a newcomer to enter and profit incentives for entry decline. The general pattern is of a process in which firms fall out of an industry from time to time as conditions change, fewer new ones enter, and older industries with reasonably homogeneous markets tend to drift slowly into a few strong hands.

The U.S. auto industry was highly fragmented in its early days but many of the companies failed or were absorbed by their competitors. After General Motors overtook Ford decisively to establish its market leadership in the 1930s the auto industry moved toward a more stable situation in which GM, Ford, and Chrysler were followed by smaller producers like Studebaker, Packard, Hudson, Nash, and Willys. Studebaker was an effective competitor before World War II, but industry economics changed. After the war the required breakeven volume had increased above Studebaker's prewar sales rate. Even after the merger with Packard Studebaker did not succeed in achieving a volume adequate to make it a viable competitor in the postwar market and eventually it dropped out. Nash, Hudson, and Willys evolved into American Motors, which has largely become a U.S. base for Renault. GM, Ford, Chrysler, and American Motors were the remaining firms in the 1960s study Reith reported.

THE NATURE OF THE COMPETITION

Markets differ significantly in whether the competition is local, national, or international, whether it comes from other sellers of the same product, of comparable products, or from entirely different material or service patterns. Two Cadillac agencies in adjacent territories compete, at least for the business of those customers who live on the boundary between them, but the Lincoln Continental competition with Cadillac is of an entirely different nature, as is that of the urban agency that promotes on-call limousine service as an alternative to owning a Cadillac or Continental.

Cadillac and Continental competed for years within boundaries set approximately by the competition of their respective parent companies, General Motors and Ford. Then Mercedes-Benz intruded, starting with a small but annually increasing percentage of this segment of the automobile market, to the point that an increasingly European design emphasis for the other two became a competitive necessity.

In a more extreme example Polaroid broke into the strong Kodak home-photography market franchise by offering instant developing, effectively segmenting the market to create an area in which only Polaroid could supply the demand. With time and the expiration of patents, however, other manufacturers have been able to enter this segment and Polaroid now has direct competition.

Competition in the Market

What is the nature of the competition in any particular market? All businesses have actual or potential competition. Also, all strategy must be viewed as competitive, considering the number of claimants there are for every available dollar of purchasing power.

In the simplest cases competition is a more or less direct issue between several business firms. Since General Motors was created Ford has been a key competitor, and as long as these two firms are important in the U.S. auto market a strong rivalry seems likely to continue. In other cases the competition has a harsher charac-ter—if one party is government-subsidized or if the national interest of a country is clearly linked with the success of a specific company—because it becomes less likely that a simple economic struggle in the marketplace can resolve the competitive issues.

Sometimes a market is dominated by competitors who are not in it but could decide to participate, because their entry potential conditions margins and competitive bids. A market may be held by only a few firms, yet suffer low margins because entry is so easy that potential garage operators control the price.

In selecting a strategy, it is desirable to characterize the nature of the competitive situation as clearly and objectively as possible. Who is in the market and why? Who is likely to enter and who is likely to leave? Why don't more people enter? Is this a national or international market? Who has a political stake in the division of market shares? Are there public policy considerations in any of the relevant countries or political jurisdictions that will override success in the marketplace?

Competitive Action Potential (CAP)

For a given business under specific conditions, who are its competitors, what are they planning to do, and how will they react to a new strategic initiative? These are key questions, not always easy to answer and crucial to the planning and action from any strategy. Most businesses and most products have existing competitors; potential competitors are everywhere and both should be considered in the strategy design. The start is to list present and potential competitors and to profile each of them. A simple competitive action potential (CAP) analysis is an effective beginning.

Competitive action potential can be derived rather easily by most groups and in a very short time. Usually there are not that many important competitors—most businesses can narrow the field rather rapidly to between two and six other firms that are the ones to watch. These firms are not unknown. Usually the management people, particularly in the marketing area, are acquainted with the managers and are aware of some of the strengths and personality limitations of the competitive firm. Given this familiarity, it requires only a brief group discussion to develop a profile of a given competitor and how that firm is likely to behave.

If the group has decided on an exciting strategy that will have a major impact on the market, when will each of the competitors learn about it and what will they do? The "when" can be guessed by the nature of the trade relationships—has "everybody" heard that a major promotion is in preparation, even though they may not know what the product is? Will competitors see product approval notices or hear reports on field tests? Most groups can guess rather accurately when their competitors will first become aware of a new product or promotion.

What can they do about it? The number of action options a given competitor has are not that large, rarely more than five or six possibilities and usually fewer. From the profile of the firm, coupled with the impressions of the group, it will be possible to rule out some of these options as unlikely or impossible; for example, if a competitor's plants are already on overtime due to production troubles that firm will probably not choose a response that will require rapid manufacture of new merchandise.

Normally a CAP analysis results in a list of two or three possible responses per competitor for a small number of key firms. This is a small enough number of possible responses for someone to spend time thinking about each of them, to decide whether any of these competitive actions have the potential for upsetting the planned campaign, and whether some slight modification might make the chosen strategy better able to withstand attack.

The initial CAP profiles are usually surprisingly accurate because an effective product and marketing team knows much more about its competitors than it realizes. Key factors can be missed, however, and these profiles merit circulation among those connected with the business as well as thoughtful consideration of the picture they present. Sometimes an information gap will become obvious and suggest further investigation. Also, familiarity with the profiles will sensitize the group to the strategic significance of bits of competitive information as they become available.

Competitive intelligence is important and in some large firms its gathering becomes a major staff activity, but at least for an initial approach a simple CAP analysis is a useful tool, and part of a sound product- and market-planning exercise.

COMPETITION: PEOPLE, PRODUCTS, AND BUSINESSES

Competitors are people and firms, but even the firm is an individual, both legally and actually, and competition is a process based on the confrontation of individuals. Too often this emphasis is lost in the impersonality of systems and approval processes. Competition is won or lost according to success in relation to other individuals. Some people may not care very much if they lose and others may respond fiercely. This is an individual matter for competition is a very personal process.

One of the advantages the Japanese have in international business is that they have been trained to think of competition in personal terms. Many western managers see competition as institutional and impersonal and sometimes get left behind when competitive issues between individual managers and individual firms become important in a given strategic situation.

Warriors as Competitors

Classicists start with Sun Tzu's *The Art of War*,[3] an interesting early work that deals largely with the psychological aspects of war. Some quotation from Sun Tzu will provide an apt and flavorful backdrop for almost any competitive business strategy.

At first Mushashi also seems remote from today but on rereading becomes a central source for competitive strategy. Mushashi was a seventeenth-century samurai. The supreme swordsman of his day, he lived out a turbulent life and died undefeated. These were not ceremonial conflicts; they ended with one combatant dead or disabled, but after establishing his mastery Mushashi stopped using a steel sword. His skill was such that the Japanese wooden swords were sufficient for him to kill all opponents. As an old man he taught a few disciples, one of whom recorded his philosophy in *The Book of Five Rings*.[4]

Swordsmanship is largely irrelevant in most business situations, but Mushashi's focus on the spirit and behavior of an opponent is not. He offers useful insights into the way in which a psychological advantage can be gained over a competitor, the way to make direct action most effective, and how to read the response a particular action is likely to provoke.

---

[3]Sun Tzu, *The Art of War*, trans. and int. by Samuel B. Griffith (Cambridge: Oxford University Press, 1971).

[4]Miyamoto Mushashi, *The Book of Five Rings*, trans. Victor Harris (Woodstock, N.Y.: Overlook Press, 1974).

Today's Competitors

Ohmae's *Mind of the Strategist*[5] is more directly useful. In addition to an interesting approach to strategy, hidden behind his insights is the same viewpoint as Mushashi's, that the competitor must be specifically identified, confronted, and defeated for success to follow. Ohmae analyzes separately the position of the corporation offering the product, the customers, and the competitors, in each case looking for a key factor for success (KFS) on which to build. Together the corporation, the customer, and the competitors form Ohmae's strategic triangle. Given a key factor for success, such as a superior cost position or a product advantage, a strategy would be developed to capitalize on it, based on exploiting a position of relative superiority, on aggressive initiatives, or on finding new strategic degrees of freedom. Ohmae gives several examples of redefining the presentation of a product to overcome a competitive disadvantage, by creating new leverages for its purchase and changing market segmentation.

Michael Porter's *Competitive Strategy*[6] focuses on market structure, competitive interaction, and the way that these cause an industry to evolve over time. He related his ideas to products with specific positioning and to interaction between products, competitors and market, and the underlying business. Market approaches could be based on cost leadership, differentiation of the product, or focus[7] on a market niche. Much of the book is devoted to typical response patterns, price leaders and followers, and changes in industry structure, integration, and maturity.

A step farther in the same direction is Sammon's *Business Competitor Intelligence*,[8] in which each chapter is written by a successful practitioner in one of the aspects of industry, market,

---

[5] Kenichi Ohmae, *The Mind of the Strategist: Business Planning for Competitive Advantage* (New York: Penguin Books, 1983).

[6] Michael Porter, *Competitive Strategy* (New York: Free Press, 1980); developed further in Michael Porter, *Competitive Advantage* (New York: Free Press, 1985).

[7] Porter uses "focus" as selection of a restricted portion of the market; here "focus" is used in the broader sense of *choosing* the desired relation to customers and market, as one would focus a camera on a near or distant objective.

[8] William Sammon, Ed., *Competitor Business Intelligence* (New York: Wiley, 1984).

and company analysis, and which offers many suggestions for the organization and control of a competitor intelligence activity. Sammon focuses on gaining a detailed understanding of the strengths and behavior patterns of specific competitors to predict what they will do next or how they may respond to a specific challenge to their sales or profitability.

The Competitive Process

All of this leads back to the underlying competitive process. Products or services are offered in the marketplace as a part of a particular mission; that is, to fill certain customer needs and at a price that permits a profit for the seller. To accomplish this the deliverable itself must be created, which may be simple or may be the result of a long innovation process. Once created, the deliverable must be displayed according to its specific needs, a focus established to form a relationship with the prospective customers, and leverages established in the minds of the customers sufficient to lead to purchases. From a pattern of related purchases a sales stream grows and the seller begins to prosper. Competitors observe the success and make offerings aimed at the same customer needs.

The issue then shifts from the simple **ability** of a product to satisfy a customer to the relative cost effectiveness of different product offerings to the same customer. Classically, the number of product offerings multiply and become more alike in character and cost; the product then becomes a commodity that the customer can purchase from the lowest priced or most convenient vendor. Some companies do well in a commodity market because they have cost, distribution, or other advantages over their competitors, based, of course, on their positions. Learning-curve theory suggests that a vendor may be able to increase the relative advantage from year to year as a result of greater production and sales volume than that of competitors.

To avoid the shift to a commodity market, marketers seek differentiation to separate the identity of their product or to fit it specifically to the needs of a group of customers in one segment of the market. In this way they create specialties, maintain higher prices, and achieve a better competitive position than in a commodity market. These firms also seek to improve their fundamental positions, whether by product innovation, vertical integration, or in any other way in which relative competitive advantage can be increased.

The day-to-day action as these processes unfold is complex and personalized between specific customers and against specific competitors. Many markets are at an in-between stage, in which various participants have successfully differentiated weak or strong specialties out of the central commodity area, yet the differentiation is small enough to require price adjustments relative to a central commodity price. The central commodity price may be set by one or more leading participants and with varying degrees of homogeneity in the industry pricing that results. When the market weakens some competitors discount below posted prices but try to keep the appearance of price maintenance to get competitive advantage from the cuts. This discounting spreads until one of the major participants cuts posted prices "to restore discipline to the market" and the situation continues to evolve from that point.

The essence is that the customer need sets a ceiling on the price, but competitive action sets the floor. Purchasing agents for manufacturers and buyers for retailers become highly expert at sensing and making advantage of the competitive interplay in which the details are a product not only of the circumstances but of the personalities of the key people and firms. Thus the products or services, the customers and markets, and the selling/producing businesses form a set that interacts continually, and this set is an essential part of the framework that should be considered in the design of strategy.

SUMMARY: LINKING STRATEGY TO COMPETITION AND MARKET

This chapter has discussed the nature of the market, the stages in the market life cycle, the nature of the competition, and the competitive process. Its purpose has been to suggest a series of market-related dimensions that must be integrated into product and business strategy for it to be effective (Figure 5.1) and as

The nature of the market

| Organization | Size | Boundaries |
| Information | Homogeneity | |

Market life cycles

Changes as the market grows

Evolution through the life cycle

Changing life cycles

Structuring the market

The nature of the competition

Competition in the market

Competitive action potential

Competitors as people

Understanding the opponent

Product and market competition

Differentiation and the competitive process

Prices: needs set the ceiling, competition sets the floor

LINKING STRATEGY TO COMPETITION AND MARKET

Figure 5.1. Market characteristics as fundamentals.

related to the overall planning and strategy to action framework in Figure 5.2. In particular, the focus was on the existence of competitors as an inevitable reality and the need to understand and confront specific individual competitors as a personal reality for anyone active in strategic management.

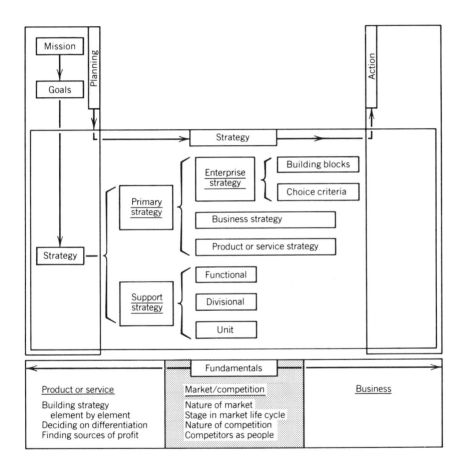

Figure 5.2. Market characteristics basic to strategy design.

6

THE BUSINESS AS THE BASIS FOR A STRATEGY

The two preceding chapters developed product and market concepts that are important as strategy is designed and put into action. This chapter extends that discussion to differences between businesses, an additional dimension in strategy design and strategic management. It begins with the business nature, life cycles, and learning curves, and then considers portfolio techniques and related management tools.

THE NATURE OF THE BUSINESS

All businesses are not the same and all strategic alternatives do not apply equally well to all businesses. The differences between them

81

are large enough so that each year *Dun's Review* publishes typical financial ratios for a great many categories of firms to help those who need to analyze their financial statements.

Accounting practices vary significantly in some business areas and can puzzle the casual business observer; for example, by the way that some public utility construction expenses increase reported current income. A rare time during its rapid growth when ITT showed symptoms of discomfort was in the integration of the Hartford Insurance Company—and insurance company accounting practices are so very dissimilar that some thought that even ITT management might have been a little confused. In the example cited earlier, Air Products, which had a highly regarded management, decided to divest Adkins-Phelps, a prospering subsidiary, because the unusual seasonal financial flows were so unlike anything else in Air Products that control of the subsidiary was uncertain.

More central to the issues of strategy design are the differences in functional emphasis in some businesses. A good commodity manufacturing strategy is often based on aiming for the lowest manufacturing cost with the greatest possible economies of scale and then trying to achieve sufficient market dominance to permit a high profit rate and an unchallengeable cost and price position. However, in a consumer marketing business low costs would not guarantee success; effective promotion would be at least as important. And a market-oriented company such as Procter & Gamble builds an important cost position for its promotion by achieving advertising price discounts based on the total advertising budget for all of its products.

These are only examples, but the point is that each type of business has its own requirements and quirks. Successful strategy design depends on an understanding of the requirements of a particular business as well as insight into the degree to which these requirements could be modified if a particular strategy called for it.

LEARNING CURVES

An important measure of business operations is their position on the learning curve. The learning-curve concept sprang from the observation that after the first prototype of a fighter plane was completed and the same vendor built a second and third plane from the same plans the cost tended to decline in a regular manner as learning accumulated.

From this initial observation and a great deal of additional study came the generalization that cost declines in a predictable way as more and more items are produced; specifically, that the logarithm of the cost of almost any operation potentially declines in direct proportion to the logarithm of the total accumulated production volume. This generalization has been confirmed in a great many different types of operations. A learning slope of 0.8 is common and both steeper and flatter slopes have been reported in specific cases after correcting the data for inflation and changes in material costs. As illustrated in Figure 6.1, this suggests that if a factory built 100 automobiles or produced 100 batches of chemicals, it would achieve a certain cost level but its costs would then fall to 80% of that level by the time that 1000 cars or 1000 batches of chemicals had been produced. These costs would decline again to 80% of the 1000-unit cost by the time that 10,000 units had been produced and to 80% of the 10,000 unit cost, or about half the 100-unit cost, by the time 100,000 units had been produced.

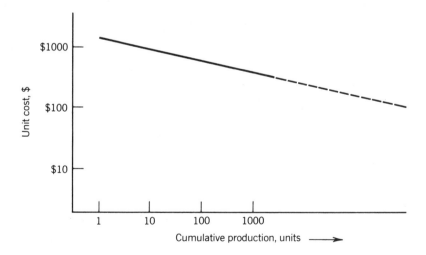

Figure 6.1. The learning curve (or experience curve).

The power of the insight that springs from this learning-curve concept is enormous, but there are limitations. The power is in visualizing the advantage of the leader in a market, who by having the largest sales volume could achieve the lowest production costs, and who should be able to increase this cost advantage steadily by continuing to manufacture and sell faster than its competitors and to move faster down a learning curve. A powerful argument can be made from this for gaining market share at almost any cost in order to get into a position in which cost advantages inevitably might appear to follow.

The problems inherent in applying the learning-curve concept are three:

1. The cost gains are not automatic. Intelligent, aggressive management is required to keep costs falling at the predicted rate, and, particularly in the dominant company, it is easy to get less gain or none at all.

2. Learning is based on making the same thing repeatedly. When model changes are small the impact may not be serious, but when changes are necessary in design and technology they may wipe out learning-curve advances entirely.

3. Learning is accomplished by a combination of innovation and teamwork and leads to a steadily improving production system. Once a system has developed to a given level it may also be achievable by others who cancel the competitive advantage by duplicating its features. Also, a system may be made obsolete if technological advances change the foundations on which the process is based.

The learning-curve concept is a highly valuable management tool, but major blunders have been caused by its careless application. Although it predicts product costs, management applications of the learning curve have been primarily as a part of an overall business philosophy, often coupled with an extreme emphasis on achieving market share. The learning curve is valuable and should be used in operations management and strategic management but as only one of a series of factors that control choice of strategy.[1]

LIFE CYCLES AND BUSINESSES

Businesses are based on the sale of products or services and have life cycles. These are based in part on the underlying product and market life cycles and in part on changes in the business itself. A research department is created to find replacements for a business's products, and its success moves that business beyond the limitations of individual product life. Markets also have life cycles and as markets mature they change. They often yield lower margins, with fiercer competition and a lower rate of major product innovations. Frequently there is a shift from a market evolution, guided by creative sellers to one with a stronger and stronger role for the aggressive buyer as the business must compete in a more difficult market.

New and fast-growing businesses tend to be profitable but to have high investment requirements. The cash-flow burden of financing growth in an exciting new market is often a heavy one and high-growth companies are traditionally cash-poor in their early years. The reason that deficit financing in these years is widely practiced is that investment requirements usually diminish as the products and markets begin to mature and cash can flow back out of the business, repay the investment, and provide a return.

Business life cycles are no more fixed than product life cycles. A firm ages as it develops and matures internally and as its relations with customers and the outside environment becomes less dynamic and more stable. If new markets open and internal

[1] Because learning curves were applied by some only to labor costs, Henderson, anxious to differentiate the services of the Boston Consulting Group, changed to the term "experience curve" as his firm explored business applications; see Boston Consulting Group, *Perspectives on Experience* (Boston: The Boston Consulting Group, 1970); see also Bruce D. Henderson, *Logic of Business Strategy* (Cambridge, Mass.: Abt/Ballinger, 1984), and Bruce D. Henderson, *Henderson on Strategy* (Cambridge, Mass.: Abt Books, 1979). For a general survey of the application of the learning-curve concept, see Robert H. Hayes and Steven C. Wheelwright, *Restoring Our Competitive Edge: Competing Through Manufacturing* (New York: Wiley, 1984).

growth resumes the business can shift back to an earlier stage in its life cycle and develop from that point. Business life cycles therefore are guides but are subject to change under the impact of an appropriate new strategy.

Several large firms have based a major part of their approach to overall strategy on the recognition that the businesses in a diverse corporation tend to occupy different stages in these cycles and need to be evaluated and managed accordingly. This concept of a business life cycle is one of the key elements in the portfolio-management approach to a comparison of businesses and business opportunities in a diversified enterprise.

A CLASSIFICATION OF BUSINESSES

From the observed dissimilarities between businesses at different stages of their life cycles in different markets and with different shares of these markets came the appealing concept of a simple system to classify them so that the best could be selected. A variety of classification systems has been tried, with some success. Although no universal system has been accepted, several approaches merit review.

The GE Stoplight Matrix

General Electric, aided by McKinsey & Company, is credited with developing and applying the simple matrix shown in Figure 6.2. Divided into nine squares, this matrix requires the classification of an industry as high, medium, or low in attractiveness and as high, medium, or low in strength.

Businesses with high- and medium-strength positions in high-attractiveness industries and high-strength positions in medium-attractiveness markets should have good profit prospects; these three squares were colored green. The yellow squares, for caution, started with a business with an excellent position in an unattractive market, a business with a medium position in a mediocre market, and a business with a poor position in an attractive market. Those businesses with a medium or poor position in an unattractive

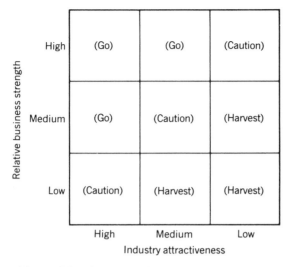

Figure 6.2. The General Electric Stoplight matrix.

market or a poor position in a medium market could have a doubtful future; the squares were colored red for "stop," and the idea was that the business should find a way to move out of the red area or GE should put it on the "harvest/divest" list and move out of that business.[2]

This simple matrix provides an excellent quick comparison but deals with almost none of the subtleties of the business positions. It is a good summary device for highlighting areas needing attention but does not provide an immediate guide to action.

The BCG Portfolio Planning Matrix

Another well-known classification matrix is shown in Figure 6.3. This four-cell matrix,[3] widely publicized by the Boston Consulting Group, classifies all markets according to high or low growth and

[2]William E. Rothschild, *Putting It All Together: A Guide to Strategic Thinking* (New York: Anacom, 1976), pp. 141–162.

[3]Malcolm B. Coate, "Elementary Portfolio Planning Models," in Thomas H. Naylor and Michele H. Mann, Eds., *Portfolio Planning and Corporate Strategy* (Oxford, Ohio: Planning Executives Institute, 1983), pp. 1–23; see also Henderson, *Logic,* and Boston Consulting Group, *Perspectives.*

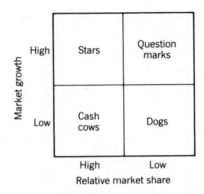

Figure 6.3. The BCG portfolio planning matrix.*

all businesses according to high or low share; the four squares are named for the most likely financial outcomes based on standard assumptions. High-share businesses in high-growth markets are stars, building importantly for the future, although investment requirements for their growth could be a cash drain in the present. High-share businesses in low-growth markets are cash cows. Investment needs should be low if market growth is past, profits should be good if the share is high, and a substantial cash flow can be milked out of the business for use elsewhere.

Businesses with a low share in a high-growth market are question marks. At some point they would become too small to be viable in relation to market growth; therefore their future is uncertain without a change in position or an investment massive enough to achieve leadership. Businesses with a low share in a low-growth market are the dogs; they are unlikely ever to generate a cash flow; better to get out of the business if that is truly the outlook.

BGC has applied this matrix widely and with a good deal of success. Like the GE Stoplight, it provides a quick classification that can be helpful and flags a standard group of management problems. Like the GE Stoplight, it does not reach the fundamentals and although it suggests problems it does so only crudely and with standardized assumptions. Judgments based on this matrix alone could go astray.

*Adapted from: The Product Portfolio Matrix, © 1970, The Boston Consulting Group, Inc.

Arthur D. Little Matrix

In reaction to the simple classification used by BGC, Arthur D. Little developed a somewhat more complex matrix for the same purpose (Figure 6.4). This matrix[4] classifies the market/industry into four categories: embryonic, growing, mature, or aging; the competitive position of the business is identified as weak, tenable, favorable, strong, or dominant. Businesses can then fall into one of $4 \times 5 = 20$ boxes; the follow-up action alternatives are also more finely classified. ADL has found the result useful, but it could still be the basis of premature action if underlying dimensions are not examined.

Refinements by Charles Hofer

To use these matrix approaches for sound management decisions requires a great deal of separate analysis of the business and its strategic alternatives. Even so, there are potential problems and to remedy one class Hofer developed an alternative matrix much richer in information (Figure 6.5). It is a 3×5 matrix in which the competitive position is classified across the top as strong, average, or weak; the vertical axis is classified according to the stage of product/market evolution as development, growth, shake-out, maturity/saturation, and decline. The additional information is based on plotting each business within the enterprise as a circle proportional to the size of the market in which it participates; a wedge inside the circle represents the market share held. Thus the users of the matrix see not only the square into which the business or product is sorted but also how large the market is and what share the entrant holds.[5]

Stages of Business Growth

Another approach to classification of businesses considers their position in their life cycles. In one system, also developed for General Electric, new businesses start at the **nascent** stage, move

[4]Coate, "Elementary."
[5]Ibid.

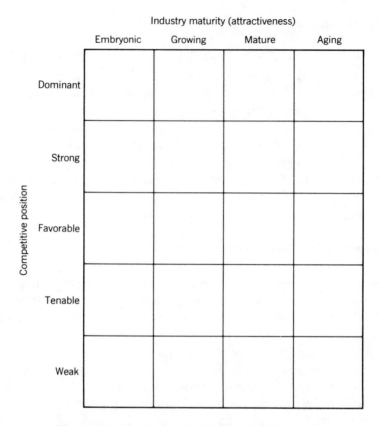

Figure 6.4. The Arthur D. Little portfolio matrix.*

into an **invest-grow** phase, then into a **mature** phase, and finally into a **divest/withdraw** phase (Figure 6.6). In the first two phases they normally represent a cash drain. Even though the invest/grow stage is normally one of high profit margins, current asset requirements grow rapidly with the business and good development of the overall potential usually requires high fixed asset investment.

During the mature phase investment requirements normally drop, profits continue, and the business generates cash that can begin to repay the investment and fund new ventures. Then, as the stage of maturity advances, profits begin to fall and the future of the business becomes less and less attractive. At some point the

*Source: Arthur D. Little Inc., "A System for Managing Diversity," Figure 1, Matrix for Categorizing Business Units, p. 8, December 1974. Reproduced by permission.

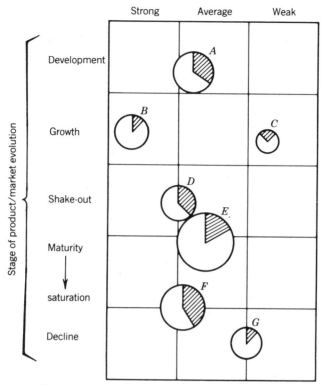

Figure 6.5. Charles Hofer's portfolio matrix.*

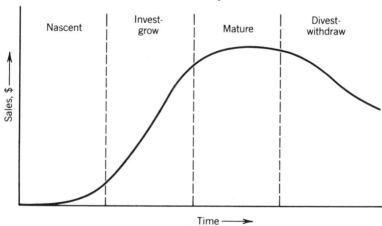

Figure 6.6. Stages of business growth.

*Source: Charles W. Hofer, "Conceptual Constructs for Formulating Corporate and Business Strategies," (Dover, MA: Case Publishing, #BP-0041), p. 3. Copyright © 1977 by Charles W. Hofer. Reproduced by permission.

harvest/divest stage is reached and management attention shifts to recovery of as much of the invested capital as possible, whether by liquidation or divestment.

These stages are real, recognizable, and useful in managing a business. However, a given stage has no fixed time span and one business may stay in the same stage of development for many years, where another will move rapidly to the later stages.

PIMS = Profit Impact of Marketing Strategy

Another interesting comparative tool is PIMS, a system developed for General Electric under the direction of Sidney Schoeffler, who then continued it as an independent effort.[6] It is not a classification but a comparative measure often used with the classification systems summarized here. Subscribers provide PIMS with confidential sales and other financial data from their operations. By compiling and compositing this information for specific lines of business, average industry data are produced and distributed to subscribers as a comparative yardstick. PIMS is widely used, particularly by longer established and more mature businesses. It can help to evaluate a business by giving management a measure of the difference between current industry average sales and profit performance and performance of their own business.

Purpose of a Classification

The idea of classifying businesses into some sort of taxonomy is to discover which to invest in, as discussed in the next section, or to manage the individual business better. As businesses pass through stages of growth and their financial characteristics change from stage to stage, both those directly in charge of a business and their superiors could benefit from an understanding of the subtleties of each situation.

General Electric made a point of the fact that a different sort of manager is required to build a fast-growing business effectively, versus maximizing the cash flow of a mature business, and that

---

[6]PIMS services are offered by the Strategic Planning Institute, 955 Massachusetts Avenue, Cambridge, Mass. 02138.

each type of manager must be measured against an appropriate set of performance standards to provide adequate incentives. This is a difficult, frontier area of using separate standards of performance for each business condition, but the need is real and a number of firms are attempting measurements and rewards on this basis.

PORTFOLIO MANAGEMENT

Portfolio management is named for the investment analogy because management of a diverse enterprise can look upon its various businesses as a portfolio. Just as a mutual-fund manager buys and sells securities, in a diverse enterprise management can use this diversity as the basis for investment and divestment decisions, shifting its portfolio of businesses in the direction of maximum opportunity for growth and profit.

This is exactly the way that a closed-end investment fund and many holding companies operate, except that an operating company can also redirect the energies of the individual business rather than just buying or selling its stock. This should give the operating management a substantial advantage over an outside investor, but it does require a considerable degree of involvement with each business to achieve that advantage.

Strategic Business Units

If management is going to judge its businesses independently according to their investment merit this requires that the elements within a large enterprise be organized as independent entities. General Electric was credited with the modern launching of this process when it broke its organization into a series of strategic business units, or SBUs—each intended to be a freestanding and more or less independent entity. The SBUs were to be given full profit responsibility based on their approved plans, held accountable for the outcome, and funded or divested according to the relative promise of each as an investment opportunity for the parent corporation (see Chapter 14). Top management guidance was to be accomplished by the interaction as the business plans for each strategic business unit were prepared, discussed, and approved and through the overall management operating system and reward structure.

The stages-of-growth type of analysis described above was one of the tools for gauging where in a portfolio of businesses money should or should not be invested. These growth stages are valuable tools because they help to emphasize the necessary shifts in business and investment management from stage to stage. Rapid investment in an invest-grow business is normal and its absence suggests mismanagement but a mature business normally requires little capital and the reasons for significant investment should be examined with care.

Portfolio management or some equivalent is a logical part of the overall resource allocation process in any diverse business and portfolio management techniques are a distinct advance. They have, however, made it easy for some managements to become remote from the underlying businesses, and the relatively poor stock market evaluation of highly diverse companies appears to reflect disappointment with the results.

A practical problem in applying portfolio management concepts in a large enterprise is the difficulty of tracking performance of a large number of business units. Haspeslagh reported the tendency of major companies to reduce the number of units considered by top management to an average of 30 by grouping them together. To a degree this defeats the purpose because the resulting top-management judgments are based on a composite of several underlying strategic business units that may have quite different profit and market characteristics.[7]

The Strategy Matrix

In some large enterprises separate strategic business units cannot be created because of the interdependencies between them, use of common facilities, and joint economies of scale. This means that these businesses cannot use the standard portfolio management

---

[7]Phillippe Haspeslagh, "Experience with Portfolio Planning: The Results of a Survey," in Thomas Naylor and Michele H. Mann, Eds., *Portfolio Planning and Corporate Strategy* (Oxford, Ohio: Planning Executives Institute, 1983), pp. 42–82.

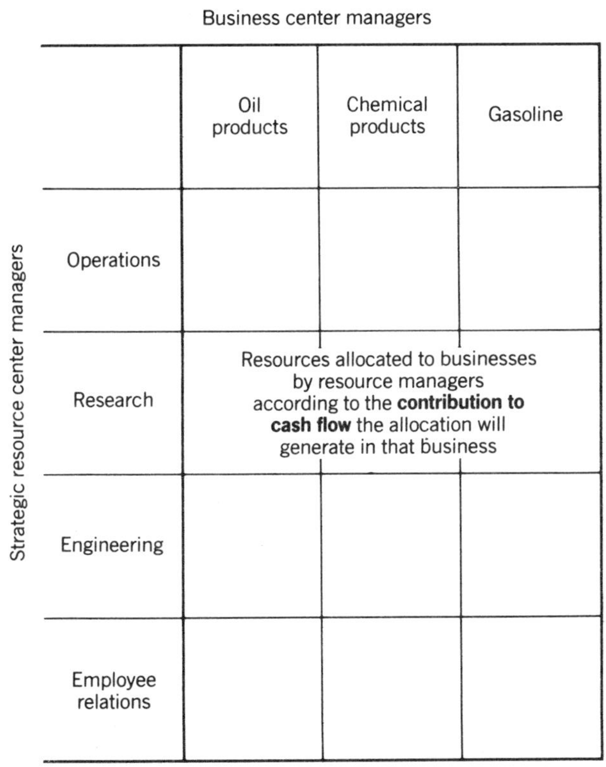
Business center managers
Oil products
Chemical products
Gasoline
Strategic resource center managers
Operations
Research
Engineering
Employee relations
Resources allocated to businesses by resource managers according to the **contribution to cash flow** the allocation will generate in that business

Figure 6.7. Naylor's strategy matrix.

approaches because they do not recognize these interdependencies. Naylor developed a strategy matrix technique for these applications[8] which applies some of the concepts that underlie matrix management to the planning problems of a diverse enterprise (Figure 6.7). In such a company business centers are organized to manage the components of the marketing activity and any other easily associated activities. Resource centers manage joint resources, such as a petroleum refinery, that distribute outputs to several businesses and allocate the output according to which business can achieve the greatest profit contribution as a result.

[8]Thomas H. Naylor, "The Strategy Matrix," in Thomas H. Naylor and Michele H. Mann, Eds., *Portfolio Planning and Corporate Strategy* (Oxford, Ohio: Planning Executives Institute, 1983), pp. 31–41.

The system of allocations is reviewed by top management during overall planning and in case of any dispute.

SUMMARY: LINKING STRATEGY TO THE NATURE OF THE BUSINESS

This chapter has examined the nature of the business and its life cycle, of learning-curve and portfolio-management concepts as a part of the necessary considerations in strategy design (Figure 6.8), and as related to the overall planning and strategy to action sequence in Figure 6.9.

The purpose of all this is to provide a prelude to the strategy-design process that follows. As developed in the first three chapters, strategy design requires a fitting together of different types and levels of strategy, as related to mission and goals. Before discussing design of strategy and the sources of energy on which it draws it is important to be clear on its foundations; a sound strategy rests on three points like a tripod, supported by the fundamentals of the product or service (Chapter 4) in its relation to the competition and the market (Chapter 5) and the business itself with which this chapter has dealt. The strategy tripod is illustrated in Figure 6.10.

Learning curves

Marching down to lower costs
Pitfalls in application

Business life cycles

Stages of growth
Changing stages

Classification of businesses

GE stoplight matrix   ADL Matrix   Stages of business growth
BCG matrix   Hofer's matrix   PIMS

Portfolio management

Strategic business units   Naylor's strategy matrix
Troubles with SBUs

LINKING STRATEGY TO THE NATURE OF THE BUSINESS

Figure 6.8. Business characteristics as fundamentals.

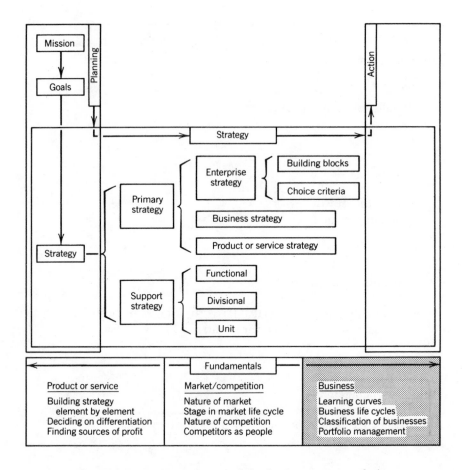

Figure 6.9. Business characteristics basic to strategy design.

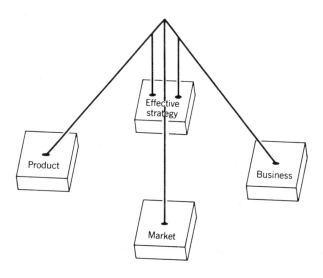

Figure 6.10. The strategy tripod

This chapter concludes the three chapters of Part 2. To this point the book has presented a framework for strategy with the three levels of primary strategy, plus supporting strategies of the component units and functions, and has related the framework to basic characteristics of the product or service, the market and competition, and the business itself. Now, with many of the basics established, Part 3 turns to some of the considerations that govern the strategy-design process.

PART 3

Designing Effective Strategies

7

SUCCESS REQUIREMENTS AND THE EXCELLENCE MODEL

Beyond the product, market, and business foundations on which a successful strategy rests are a number of considerations that determine the best way to design it to achieve the linkages summarized in Figure 7.1 and discussed in Part 3. This chapter deals with creating a necessary degree of organizational effectiveness when the successful execution of a strategy requires it. Chapter 8 discusses the strategy-design process itself, and Chapter 9 concludes Part 3 by dealing with the problem of avoiding strategic blindness and maintaining an adequate perspective of the outside world.

Some strategies are easier to execute than others. More

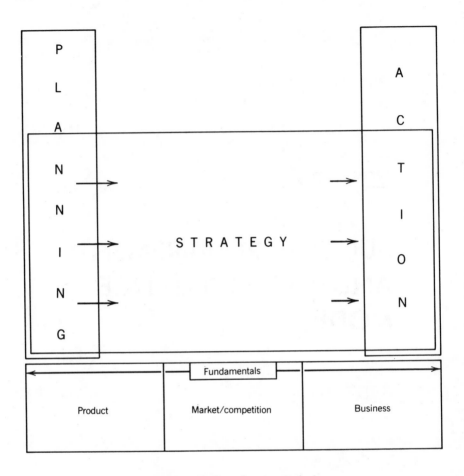

Figure 7.1. Basics of strategy design.

specifically, the execution of some strategies requires higher levels of organizational performance. Therefore it becomes important to consider the level at which a given organization can be expected to perform in relation to its competitors before selecting a strategy. This requires an understanding of the relation between the way that a company is organized and managed and its organizational performance.

Designing strategy is a little like chess against three simultaneous opponents on an extra-large board, although the individual elements of the games are not that complex, the full range of their interaction is challenging. Mastery requires an understanding of the individual elements, a procedure for assembling them into effective patterns, and a means of analyzing and refining these combinations before they can be applied, in four-handed chess or in the business world. The preceding chapters dealt with individual elements and the underlying fundamentals. This chapter begins with general considerations of assembling these elements into effective combinations and then turns to the governing role of the building-block strategies, and a definition of an excellence model for a maximum organizational contribution toward the effectiveness of a business or product strategy.

DESIGN BY RECYCLING

The strategy design process builds from the major elements discussed in earlier chapters. It requires a reconciliation of the separate requirements of product and product strategy, market and market strategy, business and business strategy, and enterprise and enterprise strategy, plus any necessary allocation and creation of resources. Complications develop because each element of strategy design depends on assumptions concerning the others. This creates a system of many simultaneous equations. Some of the variables require subjective evaluation, and solution is by trial and error compounded with judgment and common sense.

Design of product strategy requires decisions on the configuration, specifications, and costs of the deliverable and the selection of a plan for focus and display; but each of these choices requires detailed information about the nature of the market, actual and potential competition, and the competitive products' focus, positions, and leverages. When the design reaches the point of predicting competitive reaction to planned initiatives, the likely responses often require revision of the original competitive assumptions.

Sound design procedure requires continued iteration of these variables until a fully consistent set of assumptions and conclusions has been achieved. The initial assessment of market and competition, which is basically static, provides a picture of the present and the apparent trends of the future. But the idea is to design an effective strategy, the impact of which will alter the existing environment, just as do the competitive moves and countermoves it provokes. Strategy design is a dynamic process and should grapple prospectively with the same interactive and competitive elements that strategic management will encounter as the strategy is put into action.

All enterprise, business, and product strategy is competitive from the very first because every dollar from the marketplace is obtained in competition with other eager claimants. The impact of competition on strategy design is reduced in some cases, but it always exists because all products have substitutes at some level of price differentiation and any patent or other entry barrier can be bypassed if the incentive is large enough.

MAKING UP RULES

Strategy design starts with a mission and goals targeted within the span of that mission. What is this strategy intended to accomplish? From a clear answer to a few basic questions summarized in Figure 7.2 design can begin on an action program for reaching these goals. The competition in any market is governed by the established habits and customs of that market; in effect, by a set of rules. These rules can be changed and many advances have been realized by taking advantage of the opportunity to make up new ones.

Most established markets flow in smooth patterns based on the nature of the needs and the system that supplies them. In the deep, smooth-worn grooves of established practice the market leader is likely to have the advantage of ties with the distribution system and positions based on its leadership. By making up new rules for a new pattern of supply to these needs it is relatively easy to bypass the established system altogether, except that customers and various market intermediaries react instinctively against any change forced on them. Many attempts at new rules fail for this reason.

Davis & Geck once made a serious assault on Surgical Products' dominance of the surgical suture market by bypassing the surgical

What is the need area we are attempting to serve? What information have we assembled or can we get about its nature, growth, and satisfaction?

What are we offering to fill this need? What are its characteristics?

Who are our competitors? What are the competing products or services? What are their characteristics?

How will we focus our efforts on the intended customers?

From the characteristics of our organization and our deliverables, what leverages can we create? Why will our offering be preferred to the competitors? What positions can we build? What display is required? What resources will we need? What kind of cash-flow pattern will result?

What customer response and competitive response will our efforts provoke? What is the vulnerability of our efforts to competitive action or changes in the overall environment?

Figure 7.2.   Basic strategy design questions.

supply dealers, many of whom had established loyalties to Surgical Products. Selling directly to the hospitals, Davis & Geck cut its prices and improved its margins by eliminating the supply-house profit. By making up new rules for distributing sutures Davis & Geck planned to achieve market leadership. Unfortunately, however, it did not have a large enough detail force or a sufficiently comprehensive distribution system. The customers were confused by the change and did not know how to buy. Many customers continued to send orders for Davis & Geck sutures to the supply houses, which now refused to stock these products and often persuaded these customers to accept Surgical Products sutures instead. Davis & Geck had mounted its new strategy without fully understanding its support requirements, could not support it effectively, and sales plummeted. Finally it was necessary to admit failure and return to the old distribution system. The surgical supply houses were understandably hostile to a company that had tried to eliminate them, and it took Davis & Geck many years to rebuild its market position.

Making up new rules for a new way to serve the market is the best way to leap to the top. These rules, however, must be good ones, adequately supported, and the change process required to establish the new rules must be managed with sufficient skill to persuade the customers to welcome the change. In the process of strategy design it is supremely important that the design group consider imaginative alternatives to present practices. Yet it should be realistic and creative solutions should be proposed only when they can be put into action successfully.

CREATING RESOURCES

Another important dimension in the design of a strategy is any need or plan to create resources. To encourage sales of a specific product perhaps a new leverage must be established in the minds of the customers. This creation has a cost related to the effort required. If this effort builds a position, whether based on new features, lower price, brand identity, or another favorable attribute, a resource is also created. This new position can be used again and should earn rent.

The Cabbage Patch dolls were developed by a small company. Coleco introduced them nationally, using its resources to establish them in the market. By the dramatic success of this promotion a major brand position was created and the variety of subsequent Cabbage Patch dolls and accessories represented a skillful effort to maximize the rent this position could generate. Whether a created position is based on a new market franchise or a lower cost, the existence of that position invites additional efforts to achieve similar success with related products or services.

The process of resource creation needs specific attention because it has high potential and is so little recognized. Even though example after example of dramatic business success includes important created resources, business proposals are too often compared as if the money requested defined the resource need. The resource requirement is often far larger, and if a given management can truly create the other needed resources, the investment will return handsomely; if it cannot, the business will fail, even if funded with twice the requested number of dollars.

THE 7S FRAMEWORK

Resource creation often demands organizational effectiveness but the relation between the strategy and the organization has been neglected. A significant approach to this aspect of strategy design was the McKinsey 7S framework, presented by Pascale and Athos[1] and recapitulated by Peters and Waterman. As part of an internal study by the McKinsey staff, an attempt was made to redefine business basics to account for the success levels achieved by some Japanese and U.S. companies. The conclusion was that preoccupation with **strategy, structure,** and **systems** (the hard S's) had dominated the thinking of U.S. management. This preoccupation had caused a weakness in many U.S. organizations in relation to Japanese and other competitors because it caused **superordinate goals** to be neglected as well as the soft S's **(staff, style** and **skills).** The concept of the 7S framework was of seven different areas, all of which deserve emphasis. Definition of these seven S's follows.

Strategy. *Plan or course of action leading to the allocation of a firm's scarce resources, over time, to reach identified goals.*

Structure. *Characterization of the organization chart (i.e., functional, decentralized, etc.).*

Systems. *Proceduralized reports and routinized processes such as meeting formats.*

Staff. *"Demographic" description of important personnel categories within the firm (i.e., engineers, entrepreneurs, M.B.A.'s, etc.). "Staff" is not meant in line-staff terms.*

[1]Richard Tanner Pascale and Anthony G. Athos, *The Art of Japanese Management* (New York: Warner Books, 1981).

Style.   *Characterization of how key managers behave in achieving the organization's goals; also the cultural style of the organization.*

Skills.   *Distinctive capabilities of key personnel or of the firm as a whole.*

Superordinate Goals.   *The significant meanings or guiding concepts that an organization imbues in its members.*[2]

Pascale and Athos use the 7S framework as the basis of business comparisons. Their book is valuable, for many of its conclusions about past management neglect of key areas are correct. The present analysis can be considered as a parallel development in the same general field.

The reason for a parallel development is to achieve the most useful result possible. Where the 7S framework treats its seven elements as essentially equal the present definition of strategy as permitting creation of resources as well as guiding their allocation requires a broader view. Strategy is a preeminent variable. Structure becomes a derived variable except in the short run, as Chandler[3] and others suggested long ago, with systems tailored to the strategy. The mission is the genesis of a central purpose that provides superordinate or **shared goals** (after Peters and Waterman).[4] Staff and skills become two aspects of the people strategy and style equates to a considerable degree with leadership strategy. To design a strategy that not only directs but creates resources to achieve its goals, the 7S framework must be respectfully rearranged so that mission and strategy are dominant, with the other key components of successful strategy design and execution as essential but subordinate.

DESIGN OF BUILDING BLOCK STRATEGIES

The need to rearrange the 7S framework to fit the pattern of this analysis returns the discussion to the enterprise-level strategies and their effect on business and product strategy.

[2]Ibid., p. 125.

[3]Alfred D. Chandler, *Strategy and Structure* (Garden City, N.Y.: Doubleday, 1962).

[4]Thomas J. Peters and Robert H. Waterman, *In Search of Excellence: Lessons From America's Best-Run Companies* (New York, Harper & Row, 1982).

In Search of Excellence

More broadly, the issue is the way in which the governing enterprise strategies limit the performance of the organization by limiting the business and product strategies it can use successfully. Peters and Waterman approached this area from a different direction by looking for the causes of high performance. As they were careful to point out, theirs was a descriptive study of organizations based on a sample too small for statistical validation of the conclusions; but within these bounds it is very good work. The intent was to select excellent organizations based largely on objective performance criteria and then study them to see whether they had commonalities that might explain their high performance, as summarized.

The eight attributes that emerged to characterize most nearly the distinction of the excellent, innovative companies go as follows:

1. ***A bias for action*** *(for getting on with it). Even though these companies may be analytical in their approach to decision making, they are not paralyzed by that fact. . . .*

2. ***Close to the customer.*** *These companies learn from the people they serve. They provide unparalleled quality, service, and reliability—things that work and last. . . .*

3. ***Autonomy and entrepreneurship.*** *The innovative companies foster many leaders and many innovators throughout the organization. . . .*

4. ***Productivity through people.*** *The excellent companies treat the rank and file as the root source of quality and productivity gain. . . .*

5. ***Hands-on, and value driven.*** *Thomas Watson, Jr., said that "the basic philosophy of an organization has more to do with its achievements than do technological or economic resources, organizational structure, innovation, and timing." Watson and HP's William Hewlett are legendary for walking the plant floors. McDonald's Ray Kroc regularly visits stores and assesses them on the factors the company holds dear, Q.S.C. & V. (Quality, Service, Cleanliness, and Value). . . .*

6. ***Stick to the knitting.*** *. . . while there were a few exceptions, the odds for excellent performance seem to favor the companies that stay reasonably close to businesses they know. . . .*

7. **Simple form, lean staff.** *As big as most of the companies we have looked at are, none when we looked at it was formally run with a matrix organization structure, and some that had tried that form had abandoned it. The underlying structural forms and systems in the excellent companies are elegantly simple. Top-level staffs are lean; it is not uncommon to find a corporate staff of fewer than 100 people running multi-billion-dollar enterprises. . . .*

8. **Simultaneous loose-tight properties.** *The excellent companies are both centrallized and decentrallized . . . they have pushed autonomy down to the shop floor or product development team. On the other hand, they are fanatically centrallized around the few core values they hold dear. . . .*

In Search of Excellence is important reading. The wide sale of the book speaks for its favorable reception, but the study has been criticized, in part because it does not prescribe a specific pattern of organization. Heller reviewed the data presented, defended the study, and also suggested that Peters and Waterman had omitted a ninth factor at least as important as the other eight, that a serious **determination to achieve market leadership** was equally characteristic of their excellent companies.[6]

T.E.A.M.

The Atlanta Federal Reserve Bank asked a group of economists and analysts to look for common factors among 22 high-performing companies in that region. The findings paralleled substantially those of *In Search of Excellence,* to which they referred. The authors used the acronym TEAM to describe the four common factors they found:

Technology/Innovation. *A major emphasis on innovation, particularly in the area of technology.*

Entrepreneurial Management. *An entrepreneurial management style that keeps the company lean and flexible for prompt action and willing to take risks that promise high returns.*

[5]Ibid., pp. 13–15.

[6]Robert Heller, *The Supermanagers* (New York: Dutton, 1984), pp. 175–180.

Affiliation of Employees. A view of employees as associates or affiliates—the company's most valued asset—rather than as adversaries.

Market Strategy. An ongoing attention to marketing strategy that sharply defines the company's comparative advantage.[7]

Again the approach was by analyzing the behavior patterns of companies that meet other favorable criteria and without prescribing a positive course of action. This is a defensible approach. Any sample of top-notch companies deserves careful study and these companies are obviously doing a lot of things correctly.

Suppose that these companies were all using the same brand of copy machines. What would that prove? Because one or all of the excellent companies do some specific thing does not prove that it is necessary to achieve excellence. In addition to the common characteristics of high-performing companies, other information is required to synthesize a prescription for high performance, even though these studies may foreshadow most of the requirements correctly.

The Five-Fold Way

Separate from the Peters and Waterman study are a number of attempts to specify the pattern in which a successful company should operate; Allio's five-fold way is the most notable.

Successful organizations appear to endure and prosper if they develop and promote five attributes:

A dominant theme: A guiding vision, driving force, or organizational strategy toward which resources are allocated.

Organizational commitment: An endorsement of the dominant theme by all members of the organization.

Congruent managerial systems: Measures of performance, reward systems, information systems, and managerial selection procedures that fit the needs of the organization.

[7]Donald L. Koch, Delores W. Steinhauser, Bobbie H. McCrackin, and Kathryn Hart, "High Performance Companies in the Southeast: What Can They Teach Us?," *Economic Review: Federal Reserve Bank of Atlanta*, April 1984, pp. 2–24.

Functional competence: *Managers and staff who are good at their trade, be it manufacturing, finance, marketing, or any other necessary skills.*

Adaptability: *The sensitivity to change as new demands are imposed by the environment or the stakeholders.*[8]

THE EXCELLENCE MODEL

The five-fold way is an important statement, but a different approach seems to be more useful as a general guide. Central themes in all of these analyses include the importance of people and goals. As business processes have become more complex it has become more important to engage all of the people in the organization as participants in design and improvement of its programs, products, and performance. This participation is achieved only as a part of an equation based on mutual respect and interests and shared goals. For an enterprise management that will attempt complex achievements, particularly over a span of years, a broadly motivated and participating organization is an essential management tool.

People work best under simple arrangements based on direct human contact. The more elaborate and indirect forms tend to degrade into a deadening bureaucracy. A simple, personal management effort can accomplish at least as much cross-coordination as a matrix structure if the contact matrix is kept small and the managers are energetic. Organizational devices that permit this sort of direct, hands-on management become a design requirement.

The foregoing discussion can be summarized in a set of principles for a highly effective organization:

The Excellence Model

Purpose.   A clear mission for the enterprise as a whole or each part of it. Each member of the organization must come to feel a personal purpose that will contribute to the fulfillment of that

---

[8]Robert J. Allio, "Doing Well—The Five-Fold Way," *Planning Review*, January 1984, p. 4.

mission and toward which that person can devote full energy and enthusiasm.

Leadership. Active and effective leadership based on integrity and trust, with mutual respect, and sharing of ideas and enthusiasm throughout the organization.

Commitment. Work built on the shared efforts and successes of all members of the organization, with (1) high standards of performance demanded by the group more than by the leaders and standards met and exceeded by most of the participants, and (2) a level of job security, opportunity, and family security adequate to minimize distraction of group members from the organizational purpose by personal matters.

Relevance. A sharp and perceptive sense of customer needs now and as they change day by day so that the company's products or services will continue to satisfy those needs effectively.

Learning. Mastery and use of all appropriate techniques, tools, and technologies.

Excellence. A continuing drive for excellence in the quality of output, in the efficiency and effectiveness of operations, and in the determination to continue to improve each part of the organization every day.

The excellence model describes an organization with peak internal and external effectiveness of function; therefore it is the desired form wherever effectiveness of a strategy depends on superior organizational performance. This performance is achieved, enterprise strategies permitting, when a skilled and dedicated management brings about the transformation of an organization to the excellence level of operation.

The leadership and people building blocks and the choice strategies must be of a nature that will permit the excellence model to function. The individual enterprise-strategy requirements for the creation of the excellence model are summarized in Figure 7.3. Such an organization is a powerful and necessary resource for some strategies and often worth the effort of construction for the added strength and profitability of the positions it creates.

Leadership strategy: An active strategy based on respect for the individual.

Opportunity strategy: Not passive.

People strategy: Fair, caring, challenging, and creating a secure environment.

Public strategy: No specific requirement.

Resource strategy: Relaxed; organizational effectiveness makes the enterprise relatively easy to fund.

Desirability and **credibility:** Carefully conceived and enforced standards, although not necessarily rigid or formal.

Managing and **belonging:** Emphasis on areas in which the group has high confidence in its ability.

Payoff: No specific requirement, except not excessively conservative.

Figure 7.3. Enterprise-strategy requirements for maximum organizational effectiveness.

SUCCESS REQUIREMENTS AND THE EXCELLENCE MODEL

Now with a prescription for building a highly motivated organization how does this relate to strategy design? The following are some observations:

1. Not every business can or should attempt to build an organization in the excellence model. There are reasons why the U.S. Army needs a more rigid structure, which includes possible rapid expansion around the organization's nucleus in times of emergency. Many organizations are temporary; a construction contractor may draw together a crew of union members from the local building-trades council whose allegiance is to the union that places them in job after job. This makes it difficult for the contractor to create a cohesive organizational unit, particularly for a job lasting only a few weeks.

2. Not every management wishes to or is able to manage in the manner required by this organizational approach.

3. Not every business needs this caliber of organization to function effectively.

4. The excellence model describes an organization that is a valuable management tool in the pursuit of specific accomplishments. For less demanding tasks other organizational performance levels will serve, although sometimes less profitably.

SUMMARY: ORGANIZATION COMPETENCE AND STRATEGY DESIGN

This chapter has moved from the basics of strategy design to organizational excellence, how to construct it, and when it is needed, as summarized in Figure 7.4. Any given strategy requires a certain level of organization competence for its execution, a level that varies widely with the circumstances. In selecting a strategy it becomes important, therefore, to consider the requirements for its execution. When organizational excellence is required and not already established it must be created or a different strategy should be chosen.

The strategy design process

> Basic questions
> Competition
> Making rules
> Creating resources
> 7S framework

Design of building block strategies

> *In Search of Excellence*
> The TEAM study
> The Five-Fold Way

The Excellence Model

> Nature
> Value
> When to use it

BUILDING FROM A STRONG ORGANIZATION

Figure 7.4.   Success requirements and the excellence model.

8

DESIGNING A PRODUCT OR BUSINESS STRATEGY

Before actually designing a product or business strategy a review of limiting boundaries is needed. The process begins with the creation of leverages and **needs-leverages linkages**, and moves on to completion and testing before putting the decision into action.

FINDING THE BOUNDARIES

If a strategy does not fit within the boundaries already set by the organization its approval and successful execution will become more difficult. Key boundaries come from the enterprise level strategies and the territory lines around division and individual interests.

Building Block and Choice Strategies

Enterprise strategy controls many aspects of strategy design in a subtle way. The five choice criteria are applied whenever strategy is presented for approval. Their nature becomes known throughout the organization and influences the plans and proposals brought forward. Basically, the leadership, opportunity, and people strategies determine the nature of the organization itself and of the subordinate strategies likely to be favored by its management.

The opportunity building block signals the receptivity of management to specific proposals and governs a significant share of resource allocation. Likewise, the public role is an organizational attitude and posture, largely apart from individual product or business strategies.

The resources building block relates indirectly to any specific strategy. If management has easy access to funding for its projects because of good cash flow, retained earnings, or ability to create resources this gives more internal freedom in strategy design.

Enterprise Choice Criteria

The managing and belonging strategies are specific constraints. If management insists that its managers learn how to run a business before attempting to acquire it, as Johnson & Johnson has done in the past, possible acquisition areas are limited. If management rules out product areas because it does not like their connotations, as DuPont once refused to consider rest-room sanitation products, that is another sort of limit.

Credibility strategy presents a different constraint related to the way that management makes decisions. Better management requires well-thought-out proposals and capable managers to execute them, but organizations differ widely in the formality and nature of the process by which they establish project credibility.

Payoff strategy is also a constraint. If it is only a matter of meeting a preset return level, this can become a financial analyst's game of massaging the numbers until the minimum hurdle rate is met and the project can be submitted for approval. Better payoff strategies are based on balancing risk with potential for reward—although this is difficult and inevitably somewhat subjective.

Authority Limits

Will the proposed strategy challenge any organizational boundaries? Check the division lines between assignments, between delegations of authority, between the activities of different organizational units, between the zones of interest or control of specific executives, or any other sort of boundary that management may once have established or decided to tolerate. Innovative strategies often challenge boundaries and many failures are traceable to unintended challenges that were not recognized as such by the challenger. It is wisest and safest to start with a full view of the boundaries and sort out the implications of any challenges to them before putting one forward formally.

CREATING LEVERAGES

The consequences of the enterprise building block and choice strategies for business and product strategy design is a set of limits and approval criteria, clearly stated or only vaguely known, depending on the specific organization. Given some limits, then, how is a strategy designed? A simple and fundamental approach is to look for leverages. How can the business create leverages in the minds of potential customers that will lead to purchases? Of course, leverages can be defined only in terms of a specific customer need and a deliverable with the potential for filling that need profitably.[1]

How can we create leverages? When the proposed deliverable was the BetaMax, Sony felt confident enough of potential customer demands to go to the laboratory, design and build the product within an acceptable cost range, and then offer it for sale. This product had specific display requirements; most potential customers wanted to see the BetaMax, have it demonstrated and ex-

[1]Figure 4.2 contains a convenient summary of the elements of a product or business strategy and their definitions. (See 4.2 p. 46)

plained, and perhaps play with the controls themselves before deciding to buy it. This display need also led to the choice of a product focus in which Sony related to its potential customers through dealers who displayed the product. Awareness can be created by advertising, and Sony used the Dracula commercials to call attention to the product and bring potential customers into the showrooms. As its primary leverage Sony relied heavily on the basic appeal of an innovative new home entertainment system reinforced by the excellent position built by the company's reputation for dependable and innovative products.

How can we create leverages? A company may have a good product for a good market but have trouble earning a profit. Easco, a fabricated aluminum and hand tool company, invested heavily in its hand tool business over the last several years. It shifted from hot-forming to cold-forming processes with the stated objective of becoming the lowest cost manufacturer of hand tools. Long a supplier to Sears, Easco pushed aggressively to obtain other retail distribution through hardware stores and the major hardware chains. By acquisition it obtained a position in the mechanics' tool market and is striving to expand it.

Easco aims to have the largest market share in both the consumer and professional hand tool markets and the best production cost position; this would make its tool business much more profitable. The hand tool markets serve a real and growing need. With the best available scale economies in production and distribution Easco's volume should give it learning-curve advantages and positions that will allow it to grow at least as fast as the market.

Easco's initial leverages were based on the ability to supply the tools the customers wanted at prices the customers were willing to pay. This is a competitive market, and Easco's leverages had to include an adequate profit for the retailer, compared with the alternatives, and a retail price low enough to persuade most buyers to choose Easco tools over other available brands. Assuming that this strategy is executed successfully, as time passes Easco can add an ever-increasing leverage based on its position as a long-term supplier of good reputation. This is the sort of strategy that, once fully established in the marketplace, could become very profitable and run on forever.

In practice these strategies usually last only until management attention wanders far enough for new technology or complacency to allow a competitor to overtake the basic cost position or when the relation of the product to changing customer needs blurs sufficiently to allow competitors to find ways of serving the market to better advantage.

How to create leverages? As a small pharmaceutical manufacturer, Alcon chose to concentrate on the special needs of ophthalmologists, which had not been fully served by the major pharmaceutical firms. Initially the Alcon products had little novelty in a world of wonder drugs but they were superbly fitted to the way ophthalmologists wished to practice, and Alcon grew. A byproduct of this success was Conal, a division that developed a similar relationship with urologists. With rapid and profitable growth in both areas Alcon soon became large enough to discover and develop its own pharmaceuticals. Lacking a functional product advantage or a meaningful cost advantage, Alcon started by creating leverages from a focus that related closely to ophthalmological practice and tailoring its products to fit the needs of these doctors better. From essentially generic products Alcon created specialties that ophthalmologists preferred to those of their competitors. Alcon prospered.

How to create leverages? Use your positions, if they are good enough. In analyses of AT&T microcomputer offerings, some have accused that company of assuming that anything that bears the AT&T name will sell. To an extent that is true because the position that AT&T success has built will guarantee many automatic sales.

How to create leverages? A study of possible new consumer appliances led to a proposal for an electric carving knife. The deliverable could be built and the costs seemed acceptable. There was no established market because the product had never existed. No one seems to have demanded its development and many commentators ridiculed it when it was announced. Yet the developers were right; when the electric carving knife was presented as a convenience for elegant dining it found a ready market. Starting from the possibility of the deliverable, the marketers judged correctly that needs-leverage linkages could be created and then proceeded to do so successfully.

In each of these examples someone analyzed the potential deliverables and customer needs and then put energy and capital into creating that which was necessary to make the needs-leverages-purchases relationship effective and profitable in the marketplace. How to design strategy? Within the limits the organization imposes, study the potential needs-leverages linkages that could bring the level of purchases necessary to achieve the desired goals. This means matching possible deliverables against the customer needs, plus any possible redefinition of the deliverables and resegmentation of the market needs, until favorable combinations with good needs-leverages linkages are found.

Leverages are only one of the elements of strategy. A strategy must be built around a deliverable, although the deliverable may sometimes have to be redesigned to obtain the best needs-leverages linkages. Display is a product characteristic to be treated according to the product needs, as in the necessary showroom demonstration of the BetaMax. Resources are required for the effort; but resources also include positions based on past success. This leaves cash flow, the control element. In strategy design the program's cash flow should be calculated carefully; if the projected pattern is satisfactory and the resulting strategy is put into action tracking the cash flow is one good way to keep in touch with progress.

NEEDS-LEVERAGES LINKAGES

In designing product strategy, the needs-leverages linkages are the starting point. In some cases, as in the Alcon example, the leverages are broader than a specific product. An entire line of products resulted from the insights into practitioners' needs, once Alcon's focus was established. A business requires an appropriate line of related products or services and at least one needs-leverages linkage is created by an effective strategy for the line as a whole. The design of the product line should be based on a pattern of customer needs, distribution costs, or other relationships that make the members of the line more viable and profitable together than separately.

The degree to which the needs-leverages linkages for the members of a product line are common, rather than different for each product, is too variable to be generalized. The only safe procedure is to design strategies on an individual product basis, noting and accommodating the commonalities that are found, and then reviewing the overall strategy to be sure that all are appropriate and properly fitted together.

Miles Laboratories' Alka-Seltzer is an important product with a position based on a long-established market franchise. Its product strategy, however, should be related to that of Alka-Mints and Alka-Plus; by its decision to use the Alka-Seltzer brand franchise on more than one product Miles created a situation in which the needs-leverages linkages for these products are partially shared and the product strategies are best related to one another or subsumed by a program strategy for this group of three products. The same line contains One-a-Day vitamins, a product that fits into the same marketing effort but has almost no needs-leverages linkages in common with Alka-Seltzer and can be managed with relative independence.

A business strategy is based on a product or service line defined by that concept of needs satisfaction around which the business is organized. A full-line strategy is aimed at catering to every possible need of the buyer—a one-stop-shopping sort of approach—but burdens the seller with the cost of many small products and small transactions. Offering only one product or service often gives the representatives too little to attract buyer attention and too small a sales volume to make full use of the distribution system. Most businesses build to an intermediate point between a single product and an exhaustive catalog and then attempt to define needs-leverages linkages to the consumer which rationalize the whole into an attractive package.

SUPPORTING STRATEGIES

Every product or business strategy is built on assumptions about the performance of component functions or organizational units. These assumptions become goals for functional or unit performance. Preferably these goals are based on earlier planning and discussion, as a strategy is needed to achieve each functional or unit goal. The strategy design process is the same, but it is confined within the specific scope determined by the goals established by the overriding business or product strategies.

CHALLENGING ENTERPRISE STRATEGIES

These strategies are set by the parent enterprise and are often firmly fixed. Because they limit performance, they are sometimes challenged and properly so. An organization needs a routine for reexamining its overall pattern of operation, starting with the enterprise strategies. This is sensitive territory that involves the preferences of top executives.

Business or product strategy design may be poorly executed if limitations caused by enterprise-level strategies are not discussed openly because important tradeoffs are handled on a personal, subjective basis. Open discussion maintains a clearer perspective as well as establishing the significance of these limits to strategy. However, this does not necessarily mean that those limits should be crossed because they may represent appropriate boundaries for specific types of growth.

WORKING OUT A DESIGN

For a product, business, support, or enterprise strategy the starting point is information on the status quo as the definition starts. Mission, goals, and strategy for the relevant business units and for the enterprise, as well as the building block and choice strategies, should be stated, as discussed above. As a second step, consider other strategies that may be relevant and make a list of them; hopefully it will be a short list, but many strategies get snagged in approval or action because of unrecognized linkages to other programs.

When Procter & Gamble decided to market Duncan Hines cookies this automatically linked the cookie strategy with the strategies for the cake mixes and other products marketed under the Duncan Hines brand name. Although the linkage appears to be a good one, this sort of tie between product strategies reduces the freedom of product and business managers on both ends of the linkage. When the commonality is a key resource or customer group rather than a brand name the linkage may be just as important without being so obvious. This linkage is usually intended to take advantage of leverages based on an established position and may be built on the joint use of a brand name, manufacturing or distribution facilities, sales force or other resources. After looking for these linkages the designer should list any other strategies that may be affected by the one being proposed, in order to consider the degree of potential effect.

With all of this done, work can begin. If a product strategy is to be designed, choose a consistent set of assumptions, starting with the specifications and positioning of the deliverable, its degree of differentiation, and the focus, display, leverages, positions, and resources required; what will be the sources of profit? Double check the choices for consistency and begin to consider alternative values for each element.

Perhaps the nature of the assignment defines the deliverable and the focus that will be used to present it, but this usually leaves many small variations of positioning within the definition of the deliverable, plus display choices and alternatives for the use of available positions and other resources. Success requires creation of needs-leverages linkages that cause customers to purchase the product in sufficient quantity to make the effort worthwhile. Perhaps test marketing or other immediate evaluation will be appropriate until the point at which the product strategy appears to be optimum and internally consistent finally emerges.

The next check is against all of the boundaries recorded before, from other products within the organization, and from the enterprise level. If there are no boundary problems, fine; the time has come to test the strategy and to propose it formally. If there are boundary problems, what and how serious are they?

Every day management makes basic changes in boundaries laid down in the past, but more adhere to the status quo and decide not to change. In general, this is the process: define all boundaries in advance, do the best design possible, look again at the boundaries, and then go ahead according to the best judgment; that is, not taking a boundary challenge to top management unless it makes enough sense to be worth any turbulence it might cause.

ALTERNATIVES

When managers have the task of defining strategy, they usually find that a number of action programs are possible, and that each has its own set of advantages and disadvantages. As a part of the strategy design process, therefore, it is important that the alternatives be defined and evaluated.

The possible alternatives to any strategy should be listed carefully and without premature judgment, so that the manager or analyst can maintain objectivity and increase the chances of making a correct decision. All possible alternatives should be listed even if they are discarded later, because so many serious blunders come as a result of overlooking courses of action in the heat of decision. The best way to avoid this is to make a value-free statement of all of the possible choices, including that of continuing the status quo without new decisions. A value-free statement contains no judgments. It is difficult sometimes to get a group to state what it sees as a stupid alternative in value-free terms, but the effort is justified by the improvement in the evaluation process.

Given a careful list of what the alternatives really are, the decision process can begin. The first step is to discard unsuitable alternatives, but the reasons should be stated and noted in case there is any need to review this part of the process again. Reasons for discarding bad alternatives can be personal but they should be explicit: "We would never want to run the business that way!" or "That violates our goals!"

In a list of alternatives most will fall out in this sort of review. Usually only two or three possible courses of action are attractive enough in relation to the others and to the mission and goals to be worth serious evaluation. A comparison of these better alternatives often requires careful analysis of the possible costs and consequences of each.

EVALUATION VERSUS ACTION

A great many tools have been found or devised for evaluating strategies but are variable in utility because some will indicate a problem without suggesting the cause or cure; for example, market share is often a primary basis of evaluation and correctly so; in general, a larger share can be equated with a stronger position.

However, if the market share is not as high as desired the significance and corrective action cannot be directly determined. This is much like the old question of whether one should choose to be very rich or very poor. Most people would agree, given that choice, that being rich is probably better, but this does not tell anyone what to do if he or she is not yet rich. Similarly, a low market share tells management that the product position probably should be strengthened but nothing about how to do it.

In constructing a strategy, the attempt at the product and business level is to make each strategy as strong as the available products and resources will permit. Then at the enterprise level the building-block strategy points action toward the kind of enterprise management wishes to build or manage within the framework set by the mission and goals and the choice strategy sets the criteria for shifting resources and energies from project to project.

USE OF STRATEGIC MODELS

It is useful to evaluate a simple conceptual model of the proposed strategy as a means of maximizing its effectiveness and value. This model can help to improve the action plan or to make a choice between alternatives. It assists in the discovery of inconsistent elements in a particular strategy or unexpected consequences from its execution.

A strategic model is an exercise in decisions and consequences. Given that a certain strategy is to be put into action, what will the consequences be? As the action moves onward, who will be affected? Who will react and in what way? A specific approach toward developing a business should lead to a product line of a roughly predictable size and number of products and range of sales volumes; how will this work out? A given program for launching a product will lead to sales to some customers at the expense of others who may buy from someone else; is this acceptable? The idea in strategic modeling is to take the consequences of the planned actions a step or two farther than normal during the initial design of the strategy to determine whether there are surprises or inconsistencies. It is a quick, effective exercise that can show unsuspected weaknesses in a strategy while still in the design stages.[2]

Strategic modeling is a useful tool for examining, testing, and perfecting the strategy of a business:

1. To aid in the choice between alternatives.
2. To develop a better understanding of the chosen strategy.
3. To aid in defining the challenges in making it work.
4. To aid in determining whether specific decisions are consonant with a chosen overall direction or will represent a departure from it.

A given strategy has a logical set of consequences; the challenge is to recognize them in advance (Figure 8.1).

In moving from strategy to consequences, a different set of factors will be strategic to each type of business, just as specialty and commodity businesses differ. In more consumer-focused businesses distribution or the consumer interface itself may be a critical factor. A conceptual strategic model, then, is a useful analytical tool if developed from the set of strategic factors appropriate to that business.

SUMMARY: STRATEGY DESIGN

Strategy design is a straightforward but demanding pattern of laying out all the known guidelines and constraints, choosing

[2]For further discussion of strategic models see George C. Sawyer, *Corporate Planning as a Creative Process* (Oxford, Ohio: Planning Executives Institute, 1983), pp. 125–132.

I Define a proposed strategy for a product or business.

II Characterize the consequences of starting the action the strategy requires and particularly the evolution of events as the strategy has its impact, sales grow, and competitors respond.

   A How will your potential customers and competitors respond to your strategy?

      1 How well do you know your customers?
      2 How sure are you of the way they will respond?
      3 What are the major options for response from each of your competitors?
      4 Managerially, how much freedom of action will you have to shift your approach once the strategy is in motion? How tightly are you locked in? Can you use extra resources to get extra leverages if you need them?

   B What kind of business are you seeking?

      1 What focus will it require?
      2 What will its sources of profit be, as it succeeds?
      3 What sort of a product line are you building? (Number of products, distribution by size, distribution by degree of differentiation, maturity, and market position.)

   C Approximately what will the plan for your product or business look like in five years?

      1 Briefly develop each element of a business plan and characterize each of them, especially the background, environment, and functional plans.[3]
      2 Review this rough plan for feasibility, consequences, and surprises (e.g., if your thrust would take you from nothing to $500 million in five years you might have difficulty in mustering the necessary resources or in spending intelligently and fast enough to support this strategy).

(continued)

Figure 8.1. How to build a strategic model.

---

[3]See the appendix for an outline of a strategic plan and a discussion of the content of each section.

III   Turn the proposed product or business over and around and look at it from as many points of view as possible within practical constraints. The purpose is not to pick the strategy apart but to understand it thoroughly and to avoid the kind of later surprises from which business disasters are born.

IV   Keep the whole process within the boundaries of common sense.

Figure 8.1. Continued.

elements for the desired strategy, and then iterating through the elements until a consistent set is derived that can be reconciled well enough with the organizational constraints and boundaries to become the basis of an effective strategy. This usually involves the generation and evaluation of a series of alternatives and the strategic modeling technique can assist in getting a sound design. The result is then to be put forward, to be discussed, approved, and put into action.

Taken all together, strategy design is a fundamental process. Obvious in some respects, it is not always carefully practiced, and the strategy may be faulty if the design is not carefully balanced. Design can be rapid and informal as long as all elements are considered. Careful strategy design is a fundamental for the successful action that is its objective (Figure 8.2).

Finding the boundaries

Building blocks
Choice strategies
Organizational boundaries

Creating leverages

Needs-leverages linkages

Supporting strategies

The design

Alternatives
Evaluations versus action

Strategic models

BUILDING AND TESTING A STRATEGY DESIGN

Figure 8.2. Strategy design fundamentals.

133

═══9

STRATEGIC BLINDNESS

Business management does not always succeed in its endeavors. General Motors, Ford, Chrysler, International Harvester, U.S. Steel, a long list of major corporations have shown heavy losses in recent years. The frequency of difficulties and even disaster among large corporations is surprisingly high. In some cases individual managers may have made mistakes or may not have been fully competent to handle the range of issues that challenged them. In many others, however, the leaders apparently were extremely able yet their firms got into deep trouble under their leadership.

Security analysts and other outside observers often conclude afterward that these reverses were caused by the wrong choice of strategy, which raises questions about the process by which management makes strategic decisions and why it sometimes goes wrong. Even in large corporations with able managers, capable staffs for the gathering of information, and a massive pool of resources at their command this decision process sometimes yields answers that result in calamity.

STRATEGIC BLINDNESS: CAUSE AND CURE

The easiest way to explain some of the failures in major firms is to assume that for some reason management did not see or did not understand the problem; for example, it would seem that the U.S. automobile industry should have shifted to smaller, more fuel-efficient cars two to three years earlier than it did. Yet even though many people outside the industry were saying it at the time the executives concerned with this decision did not see a compelling reason to change, as demonstrated by their actions, their continuing competitive disadvantage versus the Japanese, and the heavy losses suffered by the leading manufacturers. If the auto executives had had a clear vision of the present reality, they would probably have managed their companies differently in earlier years.

Although the auto industry is a convenient target, the problem is a broader one. The same lack of perception of changes affecting an industry that the automobile executives showed is quite common. The invention which became the Xerox copier was offered to a large number of leading U.S. industrial companies, all of which turned it down. They saw a difficult and demanding technology without enough potential to justify development. Yet after Xerox demonstrated this potential and began to enjoy the profits many other companies sought to enter the market and compete for a share.

When U.S. technology led to the invention of the transistor and to its mass production for defense and aerospace applications its use in the manufacture of better and less expensive radios was dismissed by companies who were then the leading producers of radios for the U.S. and world markets. These companies convinced themselves that the transistor was not yet ready for use in consumer products.

The Japanese saw the potential. They bought transistors in quantity from Texas Instruments and other U.S. manufacturers, took them home to Japan, assembled them into radios, and brought the radios to the United States. The public was enthusiastic about the performance, light weight, and low price of transistor radios. The Japanese began to manufacture their own transistors, their radio assembly work overflowed to other Far Eastern countries, and they took over the U.S. radio market. The former leaders of the industry were so far behind by the time they were persuaded that change was necessary that they were unable to remain in the mass market for radios.

The available evidence suggests that these executives, like many other executives before and since, suffered from a condition of strategic blindness, an occupational consequence of the concentration necessary for successful operating management. It arises because an operating executive functions best from a limited viewpoint, considering only events and data with proved relevance to daily operating decisions. From this viewpoint a new transistor or a potential Xerox copier is invisible, it can have no demonstrated relevance because it never existed before.

This is strategic blindness, an operating management viewpoint limited to routine considerations and blind to everything else. Strategic blindness is not unusual. It is the **normal** condition of the operating management of any organization, until the problem is recognized and a deliberate effort is made to obtain the perspective required for strategic decisions.

PERCEPTUAL BARRIERS AND THE MEANS TO AN OVERVIEW

One of the necessary attributes of a manager is the ability to concentrate. Concentration is the process of blocking out external noises, actions, and events—to give full attention to a specific problem or situation. If a manager lacked the ability to concentrate, he or she would be shifted to a new thought or task by each interruption and would have great difficulty in finishing anything at all.

Most managers develop a considerable power of concentration, which increases as they learn to function in the hectic atmosphere of responsible operating management. This concentration is desirable; it allows them to do the job.

Concentration is also an act of exclusion. By narrowing the span of attention to the issue at hand, the rest of the world is shut out. By concentrating many hours a day for many years, the operating executive loses touch with those parts of the world beyond proven relevance to the business operation. Although the manager may have a personal life, indications are that many of the habits of concentration are carried along as an unconscious element and also applied to nonbusiness issues.

These habits take the form of a shorthand of assumptions and approximations. They allow the irrelevant to be discarded instantly and assign a specific relationship to peripheral matters so that no break in attention to the central areas is necessary to deal with them. These assumptions and approximations are usually constructed with care, but they are not reviewed—this would be a distraction—unless some external event breaks the pattern of concentration and the manager must formulate it over again. For example, early in their careers many of today's older managers formed assumptions about the relation of minorities and females to business management and some continue to use these assumptions even today without realizing how much society has changed.

Strategic blindness as described here is not uncommon. Many managers suffer from it, sometimes chronically, but it is a disease whose treatment is well advanced when the afflicted manager recognizes the problem because the solution is not difficult and most managers are eager to avoid making stupid strategic decisions.

While concentrating on operating matters a system of barriers is erected that prevents sound strategic judgment. That manager is strategically blind and risks monumental blunders by making decisions with strategic dimensions. Either these decisions should be deferred to an executive with a strategic overview of the situation or the operating executive should drop those concentration barriers temporarily and seek a strategic overview before attempting to make or evaluate strategy.

STRATEGIC OVERVIEW MANAGEMENT

A strategic overview is a vantage point from which an executive can recognize and evaluate the full range of considerations, both inside the organization and in the surrounding society, that could be relevant to the present or future significance of a particular decision. A strategic overview requires an understanding of the business of the organization and of the society around it. Much of the information regarding the external factors can be obtained from staff and other reports as long as the responsible executive who will do the evaluation is familiar with the background and has the necessary analytic and synthetic ability.

In a major shift in the upper management organization pattern at General Electric, the corporation was divided into sectors, each of which was responsible for several billions of dollars in annual sales. Each sector dealt with all of the GE businesses in one area; for example, consumer products. The sector executive level was announced as a necessary step in getting better formulation of corporate strategy. GE management felt that even though its business strategies were being well formulated, all higher level executives were too much involved in day-to-day operations to give attention to corporate strategy. The sector executives were given this missing strategic component as a primary assignment.

Other large corporations such as W.R. Grace also created sector executives, but for most firms the extra overhead of another top management level is not justified and operating executives must continue to make the strategic decisions. This does not mean that strategic calamities are necessary because it is not difficult for most managers to learn to put operating problems aside briefly and to shift to a strategic overview perspective when strategic decisions are necessary. If this shift is made routinely once a year and when urgent strategy problems arise, and if someone has anticipated the issues well enough to gather most of the information necessary for appropriate strategic decisions, strategic overview management can be handled effectively and efficiently by operating managers.

THE COMPONENTS OF A STRATEGIC OVERVIEW[1]

Strategic overview management is best given a certain discipline because it is normally performed under the pressure of time by operating managers with other preoccupations. The suggestion is for a simple pattern that will minimize the risk of overlooking important components. This pattern calls for a set of five plans in addition to the support activity necessary for informed decisions. These plans deal with social impact, opportunity, course correction, operations, and self-renewal.

Management of Social Impact

This plan deals with the consequences, the impacts on society, as the business makes decisions that affect its people, its operations, its raw materials, products and wastes, and its resources. The underlying insight is that society is profoundly affected by these impacts and is beginning to hold each business responsible for any injury or disruption its actions may cause. Management of social impact means anticipating what the firm's plan of action will mean to society, the likely reaction, and the alternatives. The intent is to operate in a businesslike and profit-oriented way, and this requires a harmonious relationship with society possible only if the business actions do not cause undue harm and disruption.[2]

The Management of Opportunity

This is a plan for utilizing the resources of the firm, first in the furtherance of its products and services, then in the evolution of its present businesses, and finally in the shift into new business areas

[1] For a more extensive discussion of strategic overview management see George C. Sawyer, *Corporate Planning as a Creative Process* (Oxford, Ohio: Planning Executives Institute, 1983).

[2] For principles and guidelines for management of social impact see George C. Sawyer, *Business and Its Environment* (Englewood Cliffs, N.J.: Prentice-Hall, 1985).

as necessary to meet the firm's goals. Although important work in the area of opportunity may be done in a research department, a strategic overview is needed for its planning and research like any other operating department often loses this perspective. A principal variable that will create new opportunities is social change and a strategic overview is necessary to follow and develop these opportunities at the correct time. The management of opportunity is discussed in Chapter 11.

The Management of Course Correction

This is a plan to keep programs from being derailed by nonstrategic changes in the world around the business. It represents the effort to guide activities to prevent a regulatory decision to ban a chemical or change a rule from causing unnecessary cost or delay (see Chapter 12).

The Management of Operations

This plan adds the insight available from a strategic overview in which the ongoing operations are adapted and changed wherever necessary so that they will continue, relevant and competitive, year after year. Emphasis is on the human component of the enterprise and the several enterprise-level strategies related to people and output. Management of operations is discussed in Chapters 13 and 14.

The Management of Self-Renewal

This is the plan for shifting people and modifying the organization to permit it and its components to strive for the immortality their legal form makes possible. This is a difficult area. The normal operating pattern already provides for qualified replacement of individual managers and other employees, one by one, as the need arises. The strategic overview helps management to judge when people should not be replaced, when they should be replaced by others with different qualifications, or when the organization structure and its operating pattern should be changed. The process is hard to manage because the critical changes directly affect the top managers who must make the plan; someone has compared this process to a surgeon taking out his own appendix. But the organization can be prepared only if its present management attempts to anticipate the requirements of the future, which will be somewhat different from the requirements of the present. Management of self-renewal is discussed in Chapter 15.

Information Requirements

Line management tends to live in the present and to decide today what should be decided today—with a hundred-year perspective if the decision seems to require it. Few line managers are willing to spend time worrying about decisions that do not yet have to be made. On the other hand, most know that when a decision is due it must be made, and they will proceed with inadequate information rather than let operations suffer for lack of direction.

When line operating managers take the time and apply the effort to achieve a strategic overview, find the need for a decision, and make it, they are likely not to have expected to face that decision at that time. Unless someone on the staff anticipated that need, the information necessary for intelligent definition and comparison of alternatives may not have been available. Effective strategic overview management requires a foresight function, a thoughtful and efficient support system for gathering information, so that when the need arises a crucial decision can be defined, intelligently evaluated, and put into action within a week or two.

SUMMARY: GOOD MANAGEMENT REQUIRES A CLEAR VIEW AHEAD

The concept of a strategic overview, which leads to a system of strategic overview management, is that for a small percentage of the time, but on a routine basis, top management of any business unit should put aside normal concentration barriers and consider all possible variables inside and outside the business. This consideration should be grounded on an adequate understanding of the stresses and changes under way in society and be well informed with regard to the consequences of the various possible courses of action. Good decisions are the products of good management, but the system of five plans suggested in support of strategic overview management helps a good management to function at peak effectiveness (Figure 9.1) and makes a strategic overview a key component in the translation from planning and strategy to action (Figure 9.2).

Strategic blindness

    Overcoming concentration barriers
    Gaining an overview

Strategic overview management

    Social impact
    Opportunity
    Course correction
    Operations
    Self-renewal

The foresight function and timely information

GOOD MANAGEMENT REQUIRES A CLEAR VIEW AHEAD

Figure 9.1. The strategic overview as a basis for action.

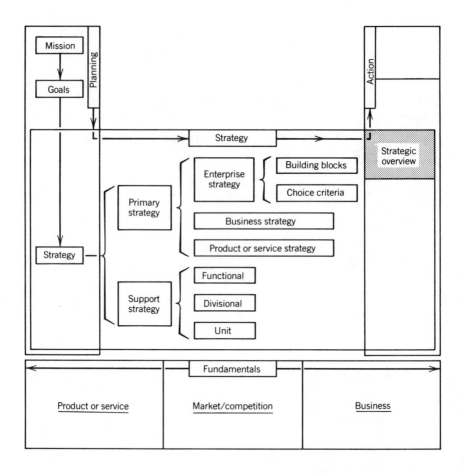

Figure 9.2. The strategic overview as key to successful action.

This chapter concludes Part 3 which began with the requirement of different strategies for different levels of organization effectiveness and an excellence model for creating the higher levels. It then considered the strategy-design process in Chapter 8 and the importance of a strategic overview in this chapter. Part 4 moves on to the management and control of the different organizational aspects, as planning and strategy move to action.

PART 4

Strategic Action and Control

≡10

STRATEGIC CONTROL

In carrying out the sequence from planning to strategy and action, it is essential that the action be keyed to a variety of requirements of the enterprise and of the environment in which it operates.

Part 4, Strategic Action and Control, consists of six chapters devoted to areas illustrated in Figure 10.1 in which requirements and actions should match; that is, the enterprise strategies and environmental requirements together determine which actions can be effective. Chapter 10 considers the impact of the individual choice criteria and their possible modification; Chapter 11 is devoted to opportunity strategy; and Chapters 13 and 14 cover leadership, people, and public strategies. Chapter 12 considers incidental interferences with strategy because an organization needs a process for avoiding them; and Chapter 15 presents the challenge of modifying the management process itself as needs change. Together these six chapters cover areas controlling the

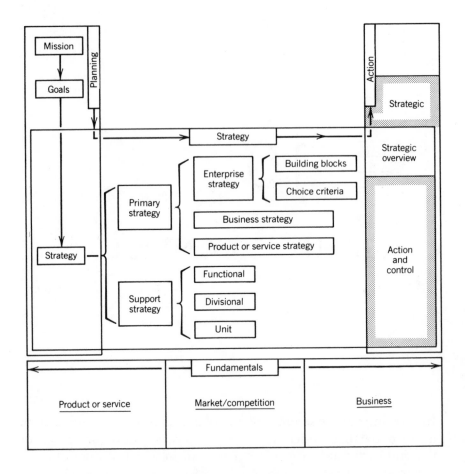

Figure 10.1. Management of strategic action and control.

translation of strategy to action where management may need to make changes if it wishes to increase the effectiveness of a particular product or business strategy. Part 4 begins with this chapter on strategic control, a key element guiding many of the others.

Just as control is a key function of management, strategic control[1] is an essential element of the flow of strategic decisions, to

---

[1]The importance of strategic control was argued by Hofer and others; e.g., Charles W. Hofer, Edwin A. Murray, Jr., Ram Charan, and Robert A. Pitts, *Strategic Management: A Casebook in Business Policy and Planning* (Minneapolis: West, 1980), pp. 19–25.

ensure that the policies being put into action and the results generated represent real progress toward the selected goals. As opposed to the control component of the normal management process which focuses on how competently policies and instructions are being translated into action, strategic control looks more at how appropriate these actions are for getting the desired results in the environment as it exists and as it will become.

The distinction between "control" and "strategic control" can be challenged on the same ground as the distinction between "management" and "strategic management," because a full and rigorous definition of "control" would have included all of this in the first place. However, actual practice has frequently left the strategic control elements unfulfilled, and the extra emphasis on a control function for strategy as well as performance is well justified.

A key part of the strategy/policy framework in any enterprise or component business is its strategic control system. This chapter focuses on the process of strategic control, beginning with a definition of the enterprise choice strategies which themselves are controls in the growth pattern of the enterprise.

ENTERPRISE CHOICE STRATEGIES

As outlined earlier, the enterprise choice strategies set criteria for decisions in the five key areas of desirability, managing, belonging, credibility, and payoff strategies.

Desirability Strategy

Although it seems obvious that the organization should engage only in what it regards as desirable activities, this area needs conscious, careful review. Sometimes it is too easy to approve individually interesting or profitable projects without considering their relation to the enterprise as a whole. The real importance of the desirability strategy, therefore, is in maintaining consistency among the various interests and efforts of the firm. The purpose is to be sure that the firm obtains the desired reinforcement and synergy among related activities, plus multiple uses of important skills, assets, or positions to maximize the rent they yield.

Strategic control over the desirability strategy is derived in a patterning by management of the intended directions of diversification and growth. This pattern should be applied as a part of the basis for project approval or rejection. Then from time to time ongoing activities should be reviewed to determine whether any component has become sufficiently unrelated to suggest redirection or discontinuance.

Managing Strategy

This enterprise choice strategy component results in a judgment of the manageability of any proposed new activity within the enterprise. This judgment is based on a pattern whose articulation describes the things this enterprise can and should attempt to manage.

The pressures on management are the contradictory forces of concentration and diversification. Diversification would seem to reduce risks, but good arguments can be made for improving results by focusing management attention narrowly on one or a few business areas. Although some managements have managed several different businesses successfully, others have failed and some hazard accompanies increasing diversity.

To the extent that management is a science it should be possible to map out the requirements of managing many businesses, plan for the necessary information and support, and operate that variety of businesses successfully from one management center. However, some businesses have elements that are not clearly understood or that change over time in a way not clear in advance, as the requirements for success in the steel business in the United States have changed over recent decades in a way unforeseen by the major steel companies, as indicated by their present situation.

Because the management of some businesses is not entirely a science, managers who have been deeply immersed in a specific business sometimes sense problems and take corrective action that could not have been taken by a more distant manager relying on the programmed art of management. For lack of this immersion, therefore, a more distant management suffers some disadvantage.

Conglomerate companies, now less favored in the stock market, tend to bring price-earnings multiples lower than their components would bring separately. Peters and Waterman[2] cite errors of excessive diversification as a performance-limiting component largely absent in their sample of excellent companies and list recent studies to show that financial performance of diverse enterprises tends to be lower than their less-diverse counterparts.

The issue for any enterprise management is that of balance. Good management of an enterprise seems more likely, all other things being equal, if that management concentrates on areas in which it has substantial knowledge of the underlying business. However, businesses and markets have life cycles, external conditions change, and the future of an enterprise may require diversification into unfamiliar territory; for example, the area of financial services is at present a dynamic and changing one. Banks, brokerage firms, and insurance companies have felt that their future was not secure unless they could broaden into a much wider range of services, and consequently their managements decided to offer different and unfamiliar financial services. Merrill Lynch moved into real estate, Prudential bought Bache to establish a base in the brokerage business, BankAmerica bought a discount broker, and so forth.

These and many other managements are attempting to move out beyond their own present knowledge of their own business because this seems to be a requirement for continuing success. Some of these moves will probably not work out well and most studies show that the failure rate in diverse acquisitions is quite high. Yet these managements decided to take the risk, and it may be that the future of some of their enterprises will depend on taking such risks and succeeding.

In selecting its criteria for managing, enterprise management is balancing at least three factors: (1) the familiar is safer and disaster due to management error less likely; (2) a given

[2]Thomas J. Peters and Robert H. Waterman, *In Search of Excellence: Lessons From America's Best-Run Companies* (New York: Harper & Row, 1982).

management group has a strength plus an individual and collective competence that varies over time; only projects that this group can manage should be undertaken; new managers can be hired to strengthen the group, but group cohesion and overall control are hard to maintain if too many are brought in at the same time; and (3) the future of the enterprise requires growth plans more than offsetting shrinkage as products and markets age, and obtaining this growth may require moving into new areas which then must be mastered and managed.

Bell Canada, the Canadian equivalent of AT&T, restructured itself in preparation for increased competition in communication and computing markets but greatly surprised analysts by buying a natural-gas pipeline company.[3] This could be a good move because the acquisition price was low in comparison with the cash flow. It projected a future in which pipeline earnings help the enterprise to keep its rich-dividend tradition while management fights for a share of the new communication markets.

Bell Canada management now has a need to understand and manage successfully in a major energy market as well as the telephone business it knows and the new markets it is entering. It has executed an attractive strategic move that made its management task more difficult. Effective management of this new area will be a success requirement. The point is not to criticize an ambitious management for an astute purchase but to illustrate the necessary balancing of programs and management abilities as the managing strategy is formulated.

Belonging Strategy

This choice strategy for comfort, fit, and controllability is a close companion of the manageability strategy. All new activities should fit the standards set by top management for belonging; that is, management should be able to feel comfortable overseeing the operation under discussion, it should mesh in an acceptable manner with the other activities of the enterprise, and it should be controllable by top management.

These are subjective standards. Comfort will relate closely to the

[3]"Bell Canada Chooses the Low-Risk Road," *Business Week*, January 16, 1984, p. 42.

manageability standards, except that a particular executive group may have a blind spot or an area of discomfort that makes management of a specific business unusually difficult. If this is not recognized the resulting mistakes may cost heavily. One pharmaceutical management was unable to adjust to the way that a successful cosmetics and toiletries business must spend money on advertising and promotion but still made several attempts to diversify into that business area. It could not bring itself to make an adequate delegation of promotion decisions to the successive general managers, and the execution of business strategy was uneven; action stopped from time to time while senior management debated whether to approve the continuing marketing program. Within the cosmetics and toiletries unit energy focused more on selling each step of its program to top management than on defeating competition and the business made little progress. Eventually the company tired of the losses, liquidated its unsuccessful venture, and concentrated its energies in other fields.

Fit may bring positives to a program if a project has the potential for sharing costs or otherwise benefiting another operation. Controllability is a subjective measure of management's ability to keep track of progress, to understand what is happening, and to know when and how to intervene if trouble develops. A part of the strength of an enterprise that contains more than one business is the potential for a business in difficulty to get help. To make this strength real top management must be aware of a problem and be able to help the business solve it.

Credibility Strategy

This is a simple strategy. No investment should be made unless top management feels confident of the quality of the plan on which the proposal is based and on the ability of those responsible for making this plan work. However, sometimes the obvious is overlooked; hence it is desirable to confirm explicit approval for quality of plan and management.

Secondary to this demand for quality is management of the consequences. Some of the rejected proposals will represent an unjustified sacrifice of opportunities. The simple solution is a second look at the rejects; if the cause of the rejection was a poor proposal but the underlying proposition is basically attractive, management should ask for revisions or look for someone else who wants to develop a sounder proposal.

Payoff Strategy

Most managements will have in mind a minimum rate of return for new projects; this may be the hurdle rate necessary to match the desired return on assets or an estimate of the company's return on capital. Beyond this is a more subjective judgment of risk and reward that becomes personal to the management group; firms sometimes fund projects with major uncertainties and this is a matter of management temperament and strategy.

Many examples and contrasts are possible. The troubles of the steel industry in the 1980s have been traced by some to management reluctance to consider new technology in the first round of post-World War II expansion; these were large, established businesses but management felt that ventures into new technology might jeopardize their profitability. In contrast, *Fortune* profiled Microsoft because of its dominant position in the software side of personal computers.[4] From the profile it was clear that this position was very much at risk; the next generation of new programs could expand and consolidate this position if well received or the company might fade back into the ranks of small software houses. Management decided to risk its future on one set of programs, yet there could have been little choice; in this industry the leader must move fast and make no mistakes. The steel industry, however, felt that it did not need to move at all.

For each enterprise there must be risk and profitability standards. If they have not been developed explicitly they will be hiding in the minds of the decision makers and influencing decisions in ways that seem obscure to observers. There is nothing wrong with subjective standards for things difficult to make objective, but for something as basic as enterprise choice strategy it

---

[4]"Microsoft's Drive to Dominate Software," *Fortune*, January 23, 1984, pp. 82–90.

is helpful to the rest of the organization to make the standards explicit.

STRATEGIC CONTROL AS AN ONGOING PROCESS

As decisions move through the management operating system, the strategic control emphasis is on evaluation of the strategy put into action versus the situation as it exists or as it will become under the impact of some new competitive development. The action of strategic control is to monitor and approve as long as the flow of strategic actions is in the desired direction or to question and review when results fall short or the environment appears to be changing. This questioning cycles the process back to reevaluation and reformulation or reaffirmation of the strategy, actions continue to flow under the new instructions, and strategic control continues to match results against them.

Competition

A first focus of strategic control is on competitive action and inaction, plus changes that influence the number and nature of potential participants in a given competitive arena. The number and strength of the competitors in the personal computer field changed rapidly in a few months, with Osborne and Texas Instruments fading from prominence and numerous new companies entering the market. The textile industry has a profound and continuing interest in U.S. relations with China because China itself, Taiwan, and Hong Kong all compete in the U.S. market on terms determined in part by the persuasiveness of the U.S. government in obtaining competitive restraint; for instance, by voluntary quotas for exports to the United States from each country. The failure of the first well in a new North Slope drilling area suggested that the importance of this oil source area might diminish as existing fields began to mature. Any competitive shift might require a recast of strategy and the role of strategic control is to signal that need.

Technology

Any new developments that represent new technology or new use of available technology could foreshadow major changes and strategic control should track them closely. Solar energy is not a factor in many energy applications because of its present high cost, but several sources report important progress with amorphous silicon systems. As this progress is carried through into commercial products and as concurrent progress in storage battery development is achieved, solar systems could become the competitive choice for many uses near the fringe of electric distribution systems. The question is how fast these developments will occur; some predict substantial near-term progress and others do not. The difference could be a critical strategic control variable for companies potentially affected.

Market Structure

Another key strategic control area is that of market structure. As product sectors grow, mature, and shrink, as competitive energies shift from one part of the market to another, and as new technologies impact, the underlying structure of a market tends to shift.

Kodak has long dominated home photography in the United States and neither the Polaroid instant camera nor Japanese competition in films has invaded this central core significantly. New technology produced video cameras. Kodak decided to offer a home video camera, thus accelerating the adoption of this new technology, and chose to enter through a joint venture with a Japanese partner. Success will shift the structure of the home photography market, and some analysts think that the shift will permit the first real competition in the central area Kodak has dominated for so long because Kodak will not control this application of video technology. This is the sort of market-structure shift that the strategic control function should follow carefully, for the strategic options available to the participants in this market could change significantly as home photography broadens into video technology.

Organizational Vitality

One of the most important strategic control areas concerns the management operating system and the overall vitality of the organization. The management operating system and the organization it serves should be a lean, responsive, effective network of linkages that helps each member of the organization to perform individual and common tasks at top effectiveness. As discussed in Chapter 14, the management operating system will atrophy and degrade spontaneously unless managed, and strategic control is the function whose effective performance will result in this management.

ENTERPRISE STRATEGY PROBLEMS

The leadership strategy of any given organization often seems to have evolved more or less by accident from the habits and behavior patterns of key managers. The posture toward opportunity and the people and public strategies also seem to develop by chance. Only resource strategy tends to get routine review as successive generations of top managers look for ways to finance their projects. In that way resource strategy is more like the five choice criteria because choice decisions must be made routinely. The criteria for the choice decisions represent a difficult area for managers of any diverse enterprise, and portfolio management and many other approaches have been suggested.

When an enterprise is formed, its management group quickly develops a style and habit patterns for their enterprise-level strategic decisions. Building-block and choice criteria developed informally become institutionalized for the future from these initial habit patterns, and because institutional change requires sustained effort by management these initial values are likely to remain embedded as organizational decision criteria almost indefinitely. Change occurs only when the chief executive officer or other major executive becomes concerned enough about one of the enterprise-level values to make an issue and a campaign out of changing it.

Enterprise strategies are not examined as carefully and frequently in most organizations as are product and business strategies and sometimes effort is misdirected as a consequence. Management neglects enterprise-level strategy for three reasons:

1. The questions from below usually do not force reevaluation of building-block and choice strategies.
2. Top management tends to be very busy on other things.
3. Enterprise-level strategy inevitably involves a certain amount of introspection to consider how well the top management itself is doing its job in that particular area. Most operating executives are not introspective by nature and tend to put off such activity.

One of the major contributions of an effective enterprise-level planning activity is that the process requires these difficult areas to be considered and a little conscious redirection from the top can often have a profound effect.

STRATEGIC CONTROL SUMMARY

The concept of strategic control is one of watching over the application of policy and implementation of strategy on a continuing basis. Where operating control monitors the efficiency and effectiveness of the action processes for the continuing operation of the enterprise and its businesses, strategic control should examine the same action processes for their strategic implications and relate them to ongoing changes in the marketplace.

These two levels of control can proceed simultaneously, but strategic control requires that a strategic overview perspective be maintained, and other control processes do not. Therefore the work of the control function divides between those portions that can be performed by operating executives in the course of their other duties and those that require some separation from routine operating pressures for effective strategic management (Figure

10.2); the latter are related to the overall planning and strategy to action sequence (Figure 10.3). Wherever this separation has not been made strategic control has usually failed, and the emphasis on it as a separate management function is in part justified by the need to link it with a strategic overview to complete it competently and successfully.

Boundaries of the choice criteria

Desirability strategy
Managing strategy
Belonging strategy
Credibility strategy
Payoff strategy

The strategic control process

Competition
Technology
Market structure
Organization vitality

The management processes

Building blocks and choice strategies
Overcoming management neglect

CONTROLLING STRATEGY AND OPERATIONS TOGETHER

Figure 10.2. Strategic control as a key management process.

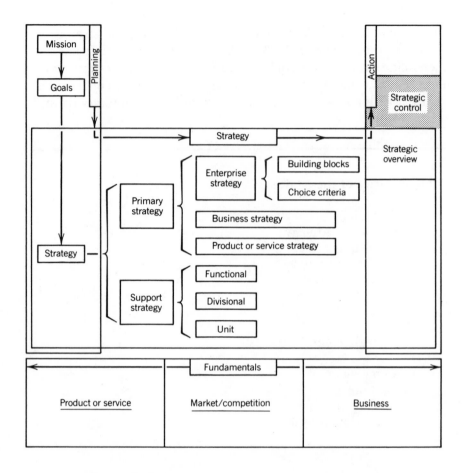

Figure 10.3. Strategic control as key to successful action.

≡11

MANAGING OPPORTUNITY

Opportunity is a key strategic component. Its shifts and evolutions are difficult to track and require a careful overview of the social, technological, competitive and other factors that influence this evolution. As discussed in Chapter 3, one of the five key enterprise building blocks is the opportunity strategy. By deciding how passive or aggressive to be in seeking out and developing innovations, how much to lead versus how much to follow others in changes in the market, and how much or little of the available talent and money to stake on new developments, an enterprise determines a major part of its organizational personality and culture, and establishes boundaries on the profit opportunities it will be able to pursue.

There is no single opportunity strategy appropriate for all

161

enterprises or even for all businesses and product areas within a diverse enterprise, but the strategy selected becomes one of the foundations to which other primary and support strategies for that organizational component must relate.

THE OPPORTUNITY PLAN

The plan for the next generation of products and businesses deals with the evolution and life cycle of the present line of products and services and the markets into which they are sold, with the growth and maturity of the present businesses, with shifts in the technology, and with investment in new businesses as required to achieve enterprise goals.

The need for an overview-level of opportunity planning seems at first to be a reflection on existing research or development units; it is not. Rather it is a realistic evaluation of the way that these and most other innovation-focused departments are formed, staffed, and operated. Usually a unit is created to achieve a set of product or business objectives and staffed with people with the capabilities required for the specific tasks. Then, as the routine operation of the unit stretches out from month-to-month and year-to-year and the unit performs the work for which it was created, these operating managers also develop their wall of concentration barriers and lose any breadth that their initial perspective may have had.

When the technical or social frontiers shift—the kind of development for which an overview perspective is often required—the busy operating manager of a research unit is as likely as any other manager to miss the significance of the shift. As a key member of a planning team with an overview perspective, however, the same manager can make major contributions as the group recognizes and capitalizes on resulting opportunities.

The Plan for New Products or Services

Products and services have typical life cycles. Chapter 4 discusses typical patterns of sales, profits, and investment. As products or services move through the life cycle appropriate to their nature, the research or development unit is normally asked to find replacement products to maintain and extend the market success. The element of overview planning in this is to try to anticipate the changes in the marketplace that will receive these new products because many markets evolve at a significant rate.

This anticipatory element needs emphasis; it is more normal for good technical people to talk to good marketing people and then concentrate on improving the present good products. Too often in the past this has led to a successful development project that has lasted for several years and produced a product obsolete while still in development because the market changed while the work was in progress. The planning should look toward developing products for the markets into which the products will actually emerge.

The Plan for the Base Business

Here the overview is focused on the evolution of the central business concept. From this central point the nature of the required products or services can be compared with what already exists. As businesses change, it is sometimes necessary to find other customer-need areas, to redefine the mission and goals, and to approach the business opportunity in a different way. AT&T promoted and accepted divestiture of its telephone operating subsidiaries to settle the Justice Department antitrust suit because this expanded its growth targets to include the national network of data transmission and related services. The need for such shifts occurs in most business areas but not frequently. Overview-level planning provides a forum in which the mission and goals of the business can be routinely reviewed, in order that when the time does come that they should be changed, managers will take notice, plan, and act.

A Plan for the Technology

Any enterprise investing in innovation processes will achieve new positions based on proprietary technology from each success. The value of these positions is reflected by the return they can generate.

Their management means realizing this return; that is, receiving the rent they can earn in their potential areas of application: to different customers, in different markets, and in different geographic areas. The management process, market by market and opportunity by opportunity, is to examine each potential application, decide whether the value is sufficient to justify development, select a development route, and get action started.

This does not mean that a firm must enter every business area, and some potentials can be developed better through other firms. Boots, a large English pharmaceutical company, discovered and developed ibuprofen. To get sales in the U.S. market it licensed the product; Upjohn marketed ibuprofen under the brand name Motrin as a prescription drug for the treatment of arthritis. Later, having established a more credible marketing presence in the U.S. prescription pharmaceutical market, Boots began to market a similar ibuprofen product under the brand name Rufen in an attempt to get more profit from direct sales than it could from its royalties from Upjohn.

At about the same time the Food and Drug Administration became convinced that ibuprofen could be sold for other purposes without a prescription. Boots, not ready for so fiercely combative a segment of the U.S. drug market, licensed the product to Whitehall Laboratories, a division of American Home Products, for over-the-counter sale. Upjohn, also aware of the potential of this market but not wishing to be identified with a product promoted in this way, licensed its U.S. rights to Bristol-Myers. The intention of Whitehall and Bristol-Myers was to obtain a substantial share of the non-prescription drug market for pain relievers dominated by aspirin and Tylenol. To the extent that they succeed, through royalties they will add to the return of the Upjohn and Boots-U.S. technical positions and ultimately to the return to the technology position of the parent Boots organization that has the basic rights to the product. This is short-term because the basic ibuprofen patent is expiring but potentially worthwhile because of the size of the market.

This situation developed because Boots was not content to earn a return from its research success only in the markets in which it was then active. It saw the potentials and obtained successful development, first through Upjohn and then through Whitehall (and, indirectly, Bristol-Myers). In the same spirit of seeking out maximum rents from any worthwhile position the research yields, new pharmaceuticals are routinely screened for additional potential as veterinary products. Substances affecting life processes of humans could also have favorable or unfavorable effects on insects or plants, and many new drugs are screened for potential in these markets. Some of the pharmaceutical companies have no veterinary sales route and many sell no insecticides or plant control chemicals, but the possible license fees are still an attractive incentive.

Shifting to Other Business Areas

Another contribution of overview analysis is as a means to better estimates of the future of the present business areas, to match the outlook for sales and profits with business goals and with returns generated elsewhere. It is not automatic that an enterprise should diversify because this increases the burden on management, but it is important that the adequacy of the prospects of the present business be estimated. If diversification offers higher returns or if the returns from the present businesses could decline, management has good reason to reexamine its opportunity, managing, and belonging strategies to determine whether entry into other businesses should be considered.

In Chapter 3 the concept of master strategy was mentioned in developing the basis for considering different levels of strategy. Master strategy carried the connotation of something more global, a superordinate strategy over the business strategies. In the governing strategies—the enterprise building block and choice strategies—one of the parts of the master strategy concept is expanded into a set of 10 characteristics given to the enterprise by management to control and shape its activities.

The other part of the master strategy concept is that of the master builder: with building blocks and choice strategies in place, to craft a major enterprise out of the complex of businesses and the pattern of investments assembled. Enterprises are built out of component businesses. If the governing strategies permit, a management able to do well in one business can build another in a related area. Thus families of businesses are created, perhaps with still others added by acquisition, subject to choice strategies to determine how similar or diverse they can be and to management skill in picking attractive areas to enter. 3M and Johnson & Johnson have built large families of closely related businesses. This relationship makes management easier and increases the chance for common use of resources or synergism in the marketplace.

At the level of overall direction of the enterprise a management wishing to build a major multibusiness company can and should be thinking about how the businesses will fit together and how the family of businesses can be expanded advantageously. This is a most proper and important part of the opportunity management plan and concept, and the tools presented here could be most helpful in the work of an entrepreneurial master builder.

OPPORTUNITY MANAGEMENT

As a part of its strategy formulation management must consider how to develop its opportunities. This involves a management strategy for the firm as a whole and an innovation strategy to guide investment in research and other creative activities.

Diversity

The managing strategy at the enterprise level specifies the degree to which the firm will attempt to manage different types of business.

Too often, unless a specific plan for managing a diversity of businesses has been developed, a firm tries to manage many businesses as if they were all the same. General Motors failed in its entry into the aircraft engine business even though it had accumulated a backlog of successful production experience during World War II. This failure has been attributed to the fact that the typical new-product development cycle for aircraft engines is many years longer than General Motors management had dealt with in its other businesses. In other ways the aircraft engine business was like the existing family of GM engine businesses, but the longer new-product development cycle required a different pattern of management.

The area of veterinary products with its attractive total dollar volume represents one of the most frequent diversification failures among pharmaceutical companies. In spite of the obvious applicability of human drug products to animal care the market is remarkably fragmented by the need to treat each species in a different way. Company after company failed because it approached the veterinary area as a simple extension of the human pharmaceutical market rather than as a family of smaller overlapping and related markets, each of which required separate service.

This is the issue of business similarity or difference that causes a management group difficulty unless it separates the businesses completely. When the businesses are completely separate, however, central management has little more than the financial statements on which to judge their progress.

Many things can change the outlook of a business before there is any reflection in the financial statement. When Exxon acquired Reliance Electric, Reliance was in the process of acquiring Federal Electric, a profitable company. Both Reliance and Exxon examined the Federal Electric financial statements and evaluated its business, but neither became aware until later that Federal Electric was about to lose Underwriters Certification for its electrical products; this caused major problems that would have been a heavy financial drain on Reliance as the acquirer had not Exxon assumed the load.

The track record of the conglomerate companies that have bought and sold subsidiaries based on financial information alone is mixed and several of the former high flyers have come to disaster. The indications are that there are times when top management needs to know a good deal about the businesses it is managing, and to the extent that such knowledge is required it limits the range of businesses with which one management can work successfully.

There is no clear agreement on how diverse an enterprise can safely be, and many different degrees of diversity are being tested by major firms. Based on this difference in diversity is a variety of control philosophies which attempt to minimize the handicap of a conglomerate company. The subdivision of General Electric, mentioned earlier, tended to create major groups in the same market areas; therefore the sector executives had a lesser degree of diversity between businesses with which to contend.

Management should consider the degree of diversity it is willing to attempt, or is required to attempt, and include this judgment as a guideline in its planning by reaffirmed or restated enterprise choice criteria. The higher the degree of diversity, the greater the risks, at least in terms of challenges to control systems and management ability. The safer course is to minimize diversity as long as this does not limit growth and profitability or introduce other risks.

Innovation.

A part of the challenge to management is the challenge to innovate. Drucker defined an innovation as a useful new combination of resources, and any management activity must deal continually with potential gains from innovation.

In particular, in the plan for managing opportunity innovation needs and plans should be laid out clearly. Many plans will consist largely of decisions to fund a certain research project and the details can be left to research functional planning, except for some composite judgment by which different projects are compared for potential payoff and success.

Other innovations require a new concept of a product application, a potential service, a means of distribution, or some other product, service, or market parameter, so that the first challenge is to generate a creative insight. The techniques for generating creative insights include structured group approaches to creativity and the use of consultants and other outside experts. At the level of the strategic overview and the plan for managing opportunity nothing limits a management group to existing inventions. A part of the overview planning process defines innovations and with surprising frequency they can be achieved if management decides to pursue them seriously.

CREATING THE FUTURE

The plan for the management of opportunity deals somewhat with the present but more with the future because in the time required to fulfill any of its plans the business will have moved into that future. The first overview specification is for an attempt to project the evolution of this future, but management is not limited to this projection. Drucker speaks of "creating the future," meaning that management has a very real power to design the future and to make it come true.

This does not mean that anything at all can be made to come true, but it does mean that new products and systems can be built, introduced, and established in the market and that distribution systems and customer habits can be shifted. RCA decided to hasten the adoption of color television and its efforts had a real impact on the rate of development. Long ago the tobacco industry launched an advertising campaign aimed at making it respectable for women to smoke cigarettes. The campaign succeeded and effectively doubled the size of the market. In neither case were the companies forcing people to do something they did not want to do—viewers wanted color television and women wanted the option of smoking—but the campaigns altered the timetable and the reality substantially.

The potential still exists for a business to influence the direction and rate of evolution of a particular trend by choosing the desired branch of that trend and hurrying its development. Thus the market is changed and the future is created to the advantage of the change agent if the campaign is carefully and thoughtfully planned. The plan for the management of opportunity starts with the momentum of existing lines and existing businesses, then looks at alternative businesses and at the future, with a challenge to management to shape that future, to create in it the opportunity it wishes to find.

SUMMARY: OPPORTUNITY MANAGEMENT

Management really has a choice of the way in which it deals with opportunity; this is a key component of enterprise choice strategy.

However, operating managers in the grips of strategic blindness are at their worst in the opportunity area because of the frequency with which the route to large advances by the enterprise or by its competitors emerges in unseen dimensions of familiar problems. Once a strategic overview is established and the enterprise and the business have created a basic posture toward opportunity—whether one of waiting for others, waiting for opportunity, seeking out the opportunity, or creating it—preparing and acting on a plan

---

The plan for managing opportunity

New products or services
The basic business
The technology
Shifting to other business areas

Opportunity

Diversity
Creating the future

The opportunity building block

Governing the innovation plan

OPPORTUNITY MANAGEMENT: TOOL OF THE MASTER
BUILDER

Figure 11.1.   Opportunity management and strategy design.

for managing opportunity is not difficult, although it requires a thorough understanding of the technical and social evolution of the surrounding environment. A sound opportunity strategy to govern the development effort determines the relative agressiveness or passiveness with which a given firm will build its plan for opportunity and put it into action. It is the key to the successful program that should follow (Figure 11.1) and continues to develop the dimensions of strategic action and control (Figure 11.2).

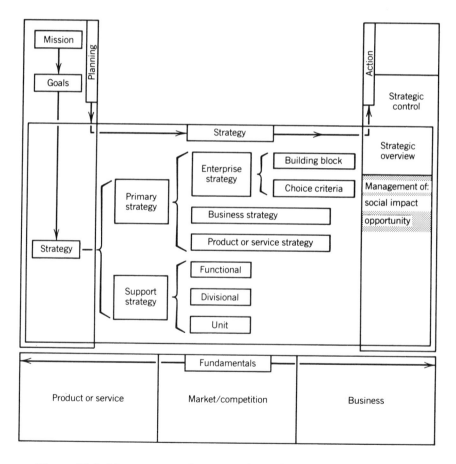

Figure 11.2. Management of opportunity as key to successful action.

12

AVOIDING POTHOLES

Just as the driver of a car or the pilot of a ship must watch for obstacles and steer around them, so must management of a business navigate through a variety of changes in laws, materials availability, and requirements. Changes directly affecting the components of a business or the essence of its strategy must be considered instantly. Many changes are essentially nonstrategic, except that affected businesses must react or conform. A change in the equal employment regulations could result in severe sanctions against a noncomplying business but has little or no effect on a business with an effective compliance process. When a hazardous chemical is banned only those using it are affected by the ban and only those without good alternatives are affected seriously.

THE PLAN FOR COURSE CORRECTION

Earlier chapters developed the manner in which an enterprise should work out mission, goals, and strategy; this includes the definition of its own building block and choice strategies, plus strategies for its businesses, products, and component functions. After all this has been well done, uncertainties of several sorts remain and continued tracking of those related to the chosen strategies will warn of any change.

However, the focus in this chapter is on nonstrategic, almost extraneous variables which are easily overlooked because they are not a part of the immediate product or the business or competitive environment. Yet they can stop a major program as abruptly as a broken axle stops a car. They are the business equivalent of the potholes drivers learn to dodge in late winter; even though they are completely impersonal and unrelated to a particular car or its occupants, they can damage a tire or break a wheel if the driver is not alert.

More than one U.S. corporation made overseas expansion plans with startup and delivery commitments and had a major program under way only to find that the needed materials did not arrive at the plant site. Construction ground to a halt. Government approvals notwithstanding, key shipments got lost in the customs warehouse; inexplicably, emergency replacements were also lost. In some countries it has been normal to make a private financial arrangement with individual customs officers to get import shipments processed. Whether this is right or wrong is not the issue here; if this is the way an official system functions, that fact must be faced. To try to move goods through an import system based on payoffs without paying the customs officials or making special clearance arrangements results in no imports. This is an example of an extraneous requirement that completely stalled more than one program because it was not recognized in advance.

The plan for enterprise course correction is a systematic, overview-level review of the direction in which the various corporate programs are aimed and the business terrain through which they must move in search of potential pothole-type hazards around which the business managers should steer.

REGULATION AND RECALLS

Major disruption of many marketing programs were among the consequences of different food and drug product recalls as the coal-tar based food colorings were screened against the modern standards of toxicity. Even though these colors had been in routine use for a great many years, some turned out to be potent carcinogens when evaluated in animals, and federal law directs immediate removal from human food or drug products of any substance known to cause cancer in animals. Companies that had long used specific colors found their products banned until they could be reformulated without the forbidden colors.

One consultant's success story dealt with Red Dye #4, one of the later members of this family of dyes to come under attack. On noting the first signs of suspicion, he prejudged the outcome and advised General Mills, his employer at the time, to take Red #4 out of all of its products. This was not difficult because other colors were available and routine marketing continued during the necessary development work. The change was made, thus moving General Mills programs away from this particular pothole. Some of its competitors suffered lost sales, embarrassment, and bad publicity because they still had products containing Red #4 in the marketplace when the official ban came.

The entire field of regulatory action is a potential source of new rules and requirements that stop programs until the firm finds a way to comply. These new rules rarely come without warning, and a part of the effort required for the course correction plan is a foresight-type review of developing regulatory themes, to determine where potential threats could be emerging.

Safety Rules

A frequent source of unexpected problems has been in new safety rules. Rules governing the transport of nuclear materials provide a convenient example. For those firms that deal with high-level radiation the waste handling is a strategic issue, but some businesses on the periphery that move only low-level nuclear materials were caught by surprise by sudden rule changes, as cities banned transport of radioactive waste and disposal site after disposal site was closed.

The entire field of hazardous materials, starting with nuclear materials and highly toxic chemicals, has become a source of great difficulty. Even "safe" and familiar materials such as benzene showed potential for causing cancer and became subject to severe new restrictions.

Safety rules must be followed, of course, and the course-correction issue concerns new rules, usually created because of a new hazard, or a new awareness of a previously unrecognized hazard. Anticipating the changes is frequently possible because the trends of investigation that produce them are well known.

The banning of Red #4 followed logically from the banning of several of its chemical cousins; that it would be tested was obvious, all of its cousins that had come under suspicion had later been banned, and from the first suspicion of cancer in the test animals the probability of an eventual ban justified the immediate action that was taken. In the same way, benzene use was not restricted at the first hint of a problem; confirmatory testing was needed and performed; alert observers knew that this testing was going on and that it was likely to lead to restrictive action long before the restrictions were put into effect.

Social Stress

When an issue is building in a community, it becomes obvious. Its potential impact on a specific business may also be discernible. A few years ago activists in several cities lost patience with the pace of federal enforcement of integration rules and instituted a series of boycotts. The targets were firms convenient to reach and surround rather than conspicuously bad actors; for example, several supermarket chains were chosen because they would be vulnerable if a boycott kept their customers away. An early diagnosis of this vulnerability might have led their managements to take extraordinary steps, not just to comply with the law but to establish a sufficient rapport with the activists that the chain would no longer be a target.

Material Shortages

OPEC caused a shortage of oil in the United States and shortages of petrochemicals soon followed. For the oil and petrochemical companies the supply and price of oil was a strategic issue. However, one small biological products business was heavily dependent on acetone, a familiar solvent used in many laboratory and production procedures for biologicals. Acetone was made from corn—at least, so the head of this business believed. It truly had been made from corn, up to twenty or so years earlier; more recently it had become a petrochemical. In a small business without staff to look at the outside environment it is not surprising that no one realized that the acetone from the local laboratory supply house was no longer being made from corn but nonetheless the petrochemical shortage caused a brief shutdown of the plant.

The plan for course corrections does not concern itself with the major, therefore strategic, materials. It does concern itself with the other materials whose flow might somehow be interrupted in a way that will disrupt business programs; for example, when a truck line goes through bankruptcy those people with freight in its system find that freight inaccessible until the remnants of the business can be unscrambled under the direction of a court.

Terrorism

In some parts of the world illegal activities pose a threat to the smooth flow of the business by the kidnapping of a key executive, or an assassination. A bomb threat can paralyze all constructive activity in a large office building for a surprisingly long time. A bomb explosion can cause injury and loss and even more disruption.

Although it is hardly possible to deal with all potential sources of irresponsible actions in any plan for course correction, it is possible to recognize areas in which the danger is higher, for example, kidnappings of American executives in Italy and one or two South American countries, and to plan operations to reduce vulnerability to this sort of interruption of the business flow.

Political Issues

Companies doing business in many countries continually skirt the political issues, not always successfully. Arab boycott rules make it theoretically impossible to do business with both Israel and the Arabs and U.S. law makes it impossible to discriminate against Israel; yet many firms have managed to keep their customers and live profitably in a market complicated by these uncertainties. Dresser Industries' French subsidiary was caught in an untenable position when the United States proved unexpectedly rigid about sales of U.S.-derived gas pipeline technology to the Soviet Union; and U.S. companies doing business in South Africa suffer periodic harassment from disapproving activist groups in the United States.

The generalization is that dealings across the borders of political systems sometimes raise political issues, some of which are clearly predictable and some unexpected. In a plan for course correction it would be appropriate to look at the potential exposure of the operation across various borders and to consider means of minimizing this exposure wherever there is significant risk.

SUMMARY: A PLAN FOR COURSE CORRECTION

The whole point here is to look around the margins of the operation for real but less obvious vulnerabilities. It is unlikely that a business would be shut down by a paper-clip strike, but if there were no paper for the copy machines it would hit some firms hard.

Not all eventualities can be anticipated and most of the time and attention should go to the strategic variables. However, a little time every year is well spent if it keeps Red #4 or an activist boycott from becoming strategic by shutting the business down unexpectedly. A large fraction of these external events that disrupt business are of a nature that their likelihood, if not the actual event, is predictable; the purpose of the plan for course correction is to reduce these interruptions of the business flow to the few truly unpredictable incidents. Figure 12.1 shows that a course-correction strategy is an important action component and it continues to develop the pattern of strategic action and control (Figure 12.2).

The plan for course correction

Regulation and recalls

Safety rules
Social stress
Material shortages
Terrorism
Political issues

KEEPING THE BUSINESS OUT OF UNNECESSARY TROUBLE

Figure 12.1.   Avoiding potholes.

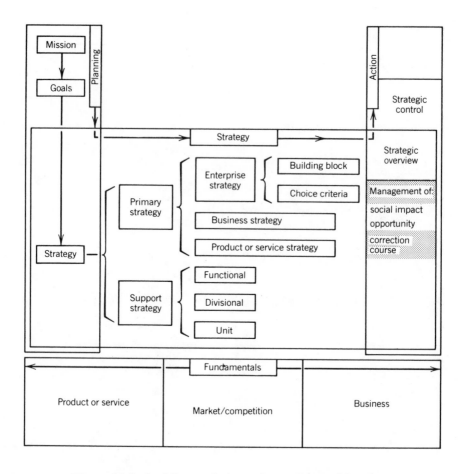

Figure 12.2. Avoiding potholes as key to successful action.

$\equiv$13

PEOPLE AND PERFORMANCE

As a component of strategic overview management, the plan for the management of operations discussed in this and Chapter 14 deals with the strategy of those operations and the strategy for managing the people on which these operations depend. These operations are directed and controlled by a management-operating system based on defined policies and operating habits of the management and by the accumulated experience of the organization.

This chapter begins with a characterization of this operating system, how management decisions become embedded in it, and the special importance of the leadership and people building-block strategies that govern the operations.

THE MANAGEMENT OPERATING SYSTEM

The management operating system is that network of linkages by which a management group communicates with its members, gathers information from organization and environment, and directs the performance of its operation. Its nature is defined by all of the policies, rules, and procedures laid down by management, plus the habit patterns developed in its functioning. Usually there is little formal design of this system—it springs up as units begin to operate and management to manage and incorporates each new directive and procedure as the enterprise evolves.

This casual and agglomerative system assembly procedure serves well because it captures decisions and occurrences and builds a library of experience that is then recalled to handle similar problems in the future with a minimum of management attention. There is a degree to which routine operating matters can be guided and decided without thought, and to this degree the automatic response of the management operating system is invaluable. This system, however, is not sufficient unto itself; like the autopilot in an airliner, it serves only to free human intelligence for larger or less routine problems. Management intelligence is needed to handle the nonroutine and to evaluate and modify the management operating system itself.

The management operating system has a set of major characteristics determined by the policies top management establishes and practices consciously or unconsciously, particularly those based on the leadership and people strategies. This system should be a dynamic, directed entity that orients day-by-day operations to the problems of today and tomorrow. Yet by its nature the system captures and stores yesterday's intelligence for reuse tomorrow.

The bridge, to keep the system alive and current, is management redirection, from yesterday to today and tomorrow. Any management operating system left to itself assumes a strong self-direction, becoming increasingly rigid in its procedures and resistant to change. Although many of its characteristics are desirable and help to keep a well planned operation running smoothly, the system rapidly becomes obsolete if a constructive and evolutionary pattern of change is not planned and directed by top management. This requires a management that comprehends the changes that tomorrow's operations will require and the practical art of accomplishing those changes smoothly so that today's operations are not disrupted. This management task requires a strategic overview for its effective planning and execution and is itself a key element of strategic overview management.

LEADERSHIP STRATEGY

One of the key enterprise building-block strategies, leadership, does more than any other variable to determine the nature of the organization. The key components of leadership style are the management attitude toward the people of the organization and the manner in which top management chooses to work with the management group and the organization as a whole.

A business organization is a group assembled for a purpose and leadership has the key role in its definition. Andrews speaks of the chief executive as the architect of that purpose,[1] and Selznick speaks of the organization as "a technical instrument for mobilizing human energies and directing them toward set aims."[2] As management directs the energies of its group toward its purpose, it uses an organizational structure whose major requirement is that it helps the group to accomplish that purpose. A part of the structure will be an organizational hierarchy or chain of command, in which those at the top direct the efforts of those below.

This is not a democratic process, for each level has a basic responsibility for the functioning of the subordinate group, but there are many ways in which each manager can choose to work with peers and subordinates. Some alternatives are formal and autocratic; others are highly participative and less formal.

Formality and Informality

A formal style of leading an organization tends toward a more uniform, rational, and controllable operating pattern and is com-

---

[1] Kenneth R. Andrews, *The Concept of Corporate Strategy*, rev. ed. (Homewood, Ill.: Richard D. Irwin, 1980), p. 5.

[2] Philip Selznick, *Leadership in Administration* (Evanston, Ill.: Row, Peterson, 1957), p. 5.

mon in large organizations, especially major government agencies and bureaus, because it minimizes the effect of individual people on organization function. For some purposes it is desirable to minimize variation created by the differences between individual people. In police and fire protection systems, for example, great emphasis is placed on a standardized response to an alarm in which there can be no hint of bias or unevenness. For other purposes, as in some research work, individual performance is required and complete standardization would be avoided.

Although a formal and standardized pattern of operation fits certain requirements it is less effective when those operations change or adapt at a significant rate. Peters and Waterman found that one of the characteristics of an excellent organization was a high degree of informality, coupled with a less elaborate organization structure and much more flexibility; instead of organizing for every contingency, a much smaller and simpler structure was modified when conditions changed.[3]

Respect for the Individual

Many years ago McGregor created the extreme organizational prototypes he called theory X and theory Y.[4] The theory X prototype was based on the concept of the lazy, undependable worker; management style and control procedures assumed this. Theory Y was a more optimistic appraisal of workers as basically wanting to do good work, cooperative and dependable if given the chance to demonstrate what they could do.

One of the most interesting things about McGregor's theory X and Y prototypes is the degree to which a given management attitude becomes a self-fulfilling prophecy guiding worker behavior into the pattern assumed in advance; that is, workers treated and controlled as lazy, dishonest, and needing close supervision react angrily to the disrespect in the viewpoint and, in that reaction, behave as badly as the theory X image forecasts. Workers treated as valuable, cooperative, and with worthwhile

[3]Thomas J. Peters and Robert H. Waterman, *In Search of Excellence: Lessons From America's Best-Run Companies* (New York: Harper & Row, 1982).

[4]Douglas McGregor, *The Human Side of Enterprise* (New York: McGraw-Hill, 1960).

opinions tended to respond favorably and are much more likely to behave according to the theory Y prototype if other operating conditions permit it.

The fundamental ingredient here is respect from one individual to another. When respect is given and received the basis is laid for productive teamwork. Peters and Waterman found that respect for every individual was a cornerstone of management philosophy in the excellent companies.[5] Certainly there are wide differences in practice from one firm to another, differences in the pattern and pace of their businesses is to some degree a factor, and the key leadership and people strategy definitions by top management have a large impact on operating results.

Shared Goals

In designing an operation management must decide how much to share with the people in that operation and some managements tell those people only what they are required to do to earn their pay. It has been observed many times in the past that the people of an organization wish to know what their work is a part of and what the goals of the effort are. Given the opportunity, they will identify with these goals and attempt to contribute to them, sometimes to a much greater degree than management has any right to expect.

Peters and Waterman identified this factor as "shared values" and reported that it was a uniform characteristic of the excellent organizations they studied; that is, excellence was linked to a leadership style in which the key values underlying the enterprise goal structure were fully shared throughout the organization and became a part of the way of life of its members.[6]

RESOURCE STRATEGY

The management-operating system draws on the resources of the enterprise as it functions, one of the enterprise building blocks is the resource strategy, and the degree of success of this strategy

[5]*In Search of Excellence*, p. 277.
[6]*Ibid.*, pp. 279–291.

effects the way the management operating system functions. Some organizations have more assets available than others, but the management ingenuity and capability in creating resources is often more important than initial funding. The resource availability influences each product and business strategy in its essence and from the positions on which a strategy can be built.

In a resource-rich organization function of the management operating system will not be resource-constrained, and the business flow will be toward committing and using those resources as rapidly as opportunities can be found that are compatible with the building-block and choice strategies. In a resource-starved organization opportunities that meet these standards will still compete for available funding and the management operating system flow will show the influence of resource shortage. Most organizations will be in some middle area; their resources will be scarce but available at a cost low enough to prevent the operation from becoming resource-starved.

Most managements frequently examine the details of resource cost and supply to find out where additional resources may be located and to consider each new funding option suggested.

THE PEOPLE COMPONENT

Another of the five enterprise building blocks is the people strategy. This is the general specification by top management of the sort of people that will be brought into the organization and how they will be treated.

Compensation and Hiring

In its approach to paying and staffing the organization top management puts a coloration on all that follows. The key decisions set the level of salaries versus competitors, the level of hiring, the internal promotion practices, and the degree of enterprise commitment to the career and security of the individual employee.

How much to pay is a key and continuing question. There is no single "best way," and good organizations have been built with different approaches. The Hoffman-La Roche U.S. organization established a policy of paying above-average base salaries as a part of its earlier organization building and used regional salary surveys and other comparative data as the basis of internal adjustments if it found that salaries for sales representatives, executive secretaries, or other payroll categories were rising in the region. The rationale was that with salaries at least 10% above industry average, plus a good bonus and benefits structure, the organization had a better choice in its hiring, got a select group from the job market as a result, could retain its people against competitive bids, and built a better and stronger organization.

Each year at graduation time there is competitive bidding for the top MBA and law-school graduates from the most prestigious schools. The salary differentials awarded these "top-of-class" graduates are surprising enough to receive feature-article coverage in the business press. The successful bidders, often management consultants or major law firms, justify paying almost a double salary to the top member of the Harvard class by the way that this enhances their image with clients.

Other firms have observed that many students with sound personal and academic credentials have difficulty in finding jobs; perhaps they do not know how to write a resume or they freeze during interviews. These firms believe that after the premium-wage offers have been made there will still be many capable graduates who will work for less if the jobs sound attractive, because they haven't had better offers. These firms make a policy of paying a little less and perhaps spend more effort on their screening process in an attempt to ensure the quality of the result.

Promotion Policies

Firms hiring many college graduates usually do so because they prefer to give them on-the-job training before promoting them to higher job levels. Other firms who wish to minimize training costs almost never hire a college graduate directly. They look instead for someone who has worked for another firm for several years, gained experience, established a track record, and can contribute immediately in a more responsible job when hired. Employees become restless, want more rapid advancement at about this point, and some are easily lured away by this kind of offer.

An organization recruited person by person from good jobs in other firms does not have the same internal ties and team spirit as a group hired and trained together. For the maximum in team building and organizational cohesiveness an organization usually hires at the entry level and then promotes primarily from within. For organizations with more focus on individual performance, less emphasis on teamwork, less career commitment to the employee, and less concern about turnover, hiring of individuals pretrained elsewhere is more common.

There is no simple answer on how much to pay or at what level to hire, but from each of the alternatives suggested comes a different pattern of internal dynamics. Pay alone is only part of the story, and the selected compensation pattern must be matched with compatible choices in the promotion and commitment dimensions and in the general character of the enterprise to get the best results from the pay level selected.

Commitment

Different organizations take different views of the commitment between employer and employee. In the past automobile firms routinely laid off workers whenever the assembly line was shut down, and when an automobile plant was closed it was more or less automatic that the workers were out of a job. IBM is an example of a different sort of firm that has taken the view that its employees should feel secure in their jobs; it goes to great length to retrain and relocate employees when an operation is closed, and to make similar employment with the company available to the workers.

Although the nature of IBM's business may make job security easier to provide than at Ford or General Motors, the auto workers objected strongly to the frequent layoffs. Step by step the auto unions won salary guarantees that made the economic burden of providing job security nearly the same for the auto companies as for IBM, but the internal relationship between company and employees was entirely different. IBM is doing something that its management committed to years ago because this was the way IBM wanted to treat its people, and its employees know it. The auto company guarantees were won only because the United Auto Workers made a strong stand for them in collective bargaining; the worker's union allegiance was strengthened as a result, even though the companies paid the cost.

Each organization evolves a policy of people treatment based on the beliefs and experiences of management and the circumstances of the business. This policy becomes a part of the framework of the organization and colors the other actions as organizational cohesion is built and the business functions. If an organization wishes to make a commitment to job security, as IBM has, to make it effective most of the promotions must come from within except in times of rapid expansion, to provide the necessary opportunities for growth of the existing employee group, and company and employees must join in some career planning to be ready to move up when openings occur.

Achievement Levels

Pay, promotion, and career planning presume that an organization is making progress in achieving its business purpose, and in theory each employee should be contributing to that progress. The people building-block strategy defines the job performance standards that the organization will impose and accept and the means by which they will be accomplished. Peters and Waterman found that their list of excellent companies had high internal performance standards and that peer pressure generated as a result of the informal leadership style and sharing of values was a greater factor than demands for performance from line superiors.

Alternatives for the leadership and people strategies vary from a theory X "police the lazy rascals" approach, or a depersonalized bureaucratic system, to the value-driven excellence model defined in Chapter 7. These choices represent a negative, a neutral, and a positive approach to the membership of the organization. Any of these patterns can get most jobs done, but the efficiency and the involvement of the members of the organization will vary from one to another, changing costs and rates of progress.

Firms in highly technical work or needing closely coordinated long-term relationships tend to gain the greatest premium from the excellence model. But McDonald's, not in a high-tech business and with a large force of young people subject to high turnover, was high on the Peters and Waterman list of excellent organizations. As at McDonald's, this management style can be carried into almost any sort of organization, but the competitive advantage it yields seems likely to be higher at a firm like 3M, where a significant fraction of the employees involve themselves in almost spontaneous design of new products and businesses.

The intent of the leadership and people strategies is to guide the development of the organization into a motivated and effective team. The motivation of people, whether workers or managers, is based on the value they can be made to see in the effort; that is, on the incentives they see. The management purpose is to cause each member of the organization to develop what Herbert Simon called an "organizational personality," in which that person focuses on accomplishing his or her role in the success of the organization.[7] Chester Barnard discussed economy of incentives, emphasizing the desirability of a blend of financial and personal motivations for best results.[8] In constructing a high-performing organization a mixture of both types of reward is normally required and the people and leadership strategies govern both reward systems.

THE EXCELLENCE MODEL AND ITS ALTERNATIVES

The people and leadership strategies must be coordinated to be effective and a requirement of the excellence model is that they be oriented toward involving every individual in a collective goal-oriented effort. This involvement is remarkably easy to achieve but it has its price.

Most people would like to believe in the importance of the effort of which they are a part and in their own ability to contribute to this effort even in a minor way. This gives meaning and justification to

---

[7]Herbert A. Simon, *Administrative Behavior,* 2nd ed. (New York: Macmillan, 1961), pp. 198–199.

[8]Chester I. Barnard, *The Functions of the Executive* (Cambridge, Mass.: Harvard University Press, 1960), pp. 139–160.

their days at work and allows a greater sense of personal satisfaction and self-worth. This desire for identification and involvement is so great that this loyalty will be given instead to a professional or fraternal organization or to a union if the management makes it difficult for the employee to identify with the company. With guidance and reinforcement from management substantial group involvement is relatively easy to generate:

1. The members need a clear understanding of the firm's mission, at least in the dimensions in which it relates to them.
2. Each individual needs to find a personal purpose within that mission; that is, to find a way in which he or she can contribute to the overall progress.
3. The group collectively needs to press against the boundaries that limit its performance and seek to improve; even though some of the group members may have little creative potential, the environment they create by their efforts and enthusiasm is heavy pressure for group performance and a remarkable catalyst for creative solutions from the group as a whole.

Steps 1 and 2 are worthwhile but less rewarding than step 3, the collective involvement of the group. This involvement of the group requires a reduction in the distractions that otherwise block it. The keys here are a sense of security for the contributors and their dependents, opportunities and rewards as earned, and scrupulously fair treatment for all individuals. This bypasses issues that otherwise preoccupy many employees, thus preventing their whole-hearted involvement and diluting group effectiveness. It also reinforces the image of the company and mission as being worth the dedication: "I take care of the Company and it will take care of me."

This group becomes fiercely loyal and expects the same loyalty in return. It sets high performance standards, sometimes higher than management would suggest, and even encourages discipline or discharge of individuals who fail group or company standards after they have had a fair chance. It expects to contribute to and share in the firm's success, at least to an extent that shows that its contributions are truly valued.

The excellence model, then, tends to produce a highly effective, highly motivated work force that requires management care and protection, in part because the potential of this group results in positions capable of earning significant rents and in part because the involvement equation has obligated management. This obligation can be a problem, in which any default may shatter the value systems around which the group has organized, and an opportunity because of the range of achievements this kind of organization makes possible.

The alternatives to the excellence model involve lower levels of organizational efficiency or effectiveness. The difference is acceptable if the strategy still has needs-leverages linkages better than competitive offerings and the firm is still able to prosper. Sometimes a management astute in its grasp of the market situation will make rules well enough and find needs-leverages linkages good enough to permit it to prosper without having a good organization at all—someone who is smart enough or lucky enough does not have to do everything else in the best possible way. Unless one can plan on never meeting a smarter or luckier operator, for the long run it seems wise to build the best possible operating unit to capture as many advantages as possible.

SUMMARY: PEOPLE AS A COMPONENT IN ENTERPRISE OPERATIONS

The enterprise is managed by a management operating system and many of the most important decisions top management makes are those that determine the nature of that system and the linkages between groups and between people on which this system is built. These decisions will be an expression of the leadership strategy that has been selected and the people strategy of the enterprise. Together they will determine much of the character of the organization, perhaps including the businesses it can and cannot enter successfully. The people strategy for enterprise operations is a key input for strategy and action design (Figure 13-1).

The management operating system

Leadership strategy

Formality and informality
Respect for the individual
Shared goals

Resource strategy

The people component

Compensation and hiring
Promotion policies
Commitment
Achievement levels

The excellence model and its alternatives

PEOPLE AS A KEY COMPONENT IN ENTERPRISE STRATEGY

Figure 13.1. People and Performance.

193

The importance of this people component in operations is both absolute and comparative. In an absolute sense there is no operation at all without the people to staff it. In a comparative sense the operation runs well or less well according to the abilities and enthusiasm of the individuals and the effectiveness of the management operating system that links them. By choices of the governing enterprise strategies, therefore, and in its oversight of the management operating system management can establish a level of contribution effectiveness from its investment in people. This level is a critical variable in design of many business and product strategies and a key component of strategic action and control (Figure 13.2).

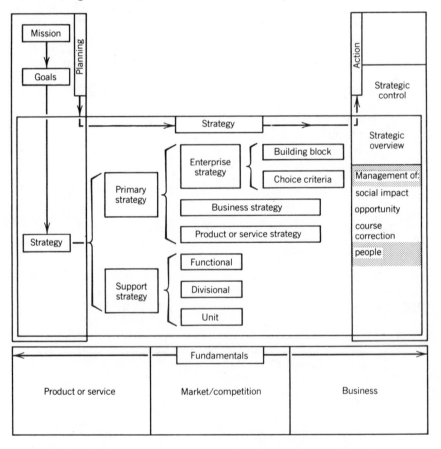

Figure 13.2. Management of people as key to successful action.

≡14

OPERATIONS, DAY BY DAY

Enterprise operations must be mapped out in general and then in specific terms, as discussed in Chapter 13, but this planning becomes real only in the day-to-day, as operations go on. This chapter examines organization of the enterprise into operating units as well as its public strategy. It then considers the design philosophy underlying the structure of the work, its application to white-collar and blue-collar operations, and the options for support strategy as various functional elements define their role in carrying out the primary strategies to which their efforts contribute.

ORGANIZING THE ENTERPRISE

A firm with many products must usually separate their management. Control over different processes, different technologies, and different customer groups calls for different management responsibilities within the firm. The intricacy of this management problem varies from firm to firm, and the managing and belonging strategies establish how complex and diverse a given company's operations will be allowed to become.

As any significant degree of diversity is established, its management should be structured. Firms operating in several business areas often organize their operations into strategic business units, or SBUs, by following the pattern once set by General Electric. Each SBU is normally intended to be an independent business that controls the resources necessary for its function and operates more or less autonomously under the oversight of upper management.

The SBUs are often gathered into groups, with a convenient number of SBUs reporting to a group executive, a convenient number of group executives reporting to a more senior executive, and so forth, until all of the SBUs of a large enterprise are assembled into a hierarchy. This model has limitations; as discussed in Chapter 6, one problem is that senior management can give proper attention to the fundamentals of only a limited number of businesses. In some large organizations top management reviews the planning and strategy only of groups of businesses, and senior executives then have little direct contact with the individual operations whose needs-leverages linkages sustain and expand the firm. The General Electric solution to this and other structural problems was to break the firm into five sectors, in which each executive was responsible for the strategy of a sector and the businesses within it; by dealing with only one-fifth of the corporation a more direct management of its businesses could be accomplished.

Also, the assumption of total independence of the SBUs is weak, a condition that is hard to compensate. Many firms assemble their businesses because of common technologies, common customer groups, or other relationships that often make them reinforce one another. Yet the pressure of the SBU framework tends to prevent general managers from acknowledging these relationships and acting on the commonalities unless it improves the short-term profits of their individual SBUs. Left to itself, this pressure destroys the synergism between the businesses.

Also, many SBUs are not given full control of their resources. A major plant complex or refinery may need to be run as an integrated unit, yet may supply products for several businesses, a distribution system may serve several businesses selling in the same region or to the same customers, or there may be still other good reasons to use shared resources. Yet this resource sharing to a degree defeats the performance measurement concept of the SBU. As discussed in Chapter 6, Naylor suggested a strategy matrix system of product and resource centers to be used when SBU definitions become artificial.

The central organizational requirements of the enterprise are actually rather simple, in spite of these complexities. Separate business operations should each be under the control of executives who plan and execute the strategy and who are accountable for and rewarded according to the outcome. Each of these separate operations should be within the personal oversight and control of a more senior manager, and the resulting enterprise hierarchy requires sufficient organizational cohesion to insure coordination and common purpose.

Within the business units, and to a degree at the enterprise level, structure must follow strategy. In the short term a given structure limits the strategies a unit can execute, but in the long run either strategy prevails and the structure evolves, or the unit begins to lose competitive effectiveness as conditions change.

The major structuring alternatives of large organizations all fight the same dilemma:

1. To organize in a way that **guarantees** the desired coordination and control as an automatic part of the management operating system creates a formal structure which then becomes bureaucratic and impersonal.

2. To maintain the necessary personal relationships between managers leaves the coordination and control on an informal basis that in a large organization eventually fails.

The solution to this dilemma and the pattern required by the excellence model is to keep the effective size of the organization small enough so that personal control can be maintained. The variety of mechanisms for keeping the organization small break it into parts and coordinate them. The Johnson & Johnson solution is perhaps the most elegant structurally, in that the parent corporation keeps its organization small by creating a new subsidiary for each business entity. This subsidiary has its own officers and board of directors to run it and needs no other reporting relationships. It owns its own resources or obtains them by negotiated contracts with other corporations. Those chosen for the board of directors of a subsidiary are usually officers of related J & J subsidiaries. The directors coordinate the efforts of the different business, and they have a personal interest in making the coordination effective.

Other firms keep unit size down by subdividing operations when they reach what is viewed as a critical size and by avoiding almost entirely the central staff functions typical of a large firm. This lack of central staff enforces decentralization of routine decisions to lower management levels, and the top management needs extensive personal contact to maintain control without heavy staff assistance. These companies tend to be "management by walking around" types in which senior executives spend heavily of their time in keeping contact with the people and operations reporting to them. In Pascale and Althos' profile of Matsushita[1] and Auletta's profile of Riboud,[2] both CEOs of extremely successful multibillion-dollar companies, the authors emphasized that these two men spent a large part of their time on managerial selection decisions and on maintaining contact with individual managers; the missions and value systems of their firms were already established and putting the right people in the right places was a more important use of their time than tracking every business decision.

Not all firms will choose to create units small enough to be managed in the pattern of the excellence model. Not all managers

[1]Richard Tanner Pascale and Anthony G. Athos, *The Art of Japanese Management: Applications for American Executives* (New York: Simon & Schuster, 1981).

[2]Ken Auletta, *The Art of Corporate Success: The Story of Schlumberger* (New York: Putnam, 1984).

could manage in this style or would be comfortable in doing so; many organizations are operating strategies now sufficiently effective and profitable that they are under no pressure to change and some managements believe that there are other routes to success. General Electric, as an example, would appear to be too large in its central functions and in some of its operating units to fit the norms suggested by the *In Search of Excellence* study. Yet General Electric has had a long uninterrupted period of growth; successive managements have experimented quite successfully as they searched for the best means for the central planning and control of a large and diverse enterprise.

When management chooses a more elaborate and more formal central means of coordination, there is normally a tradeoff in that that management no longer can be so personal, and the impersonality normally is followed by poorer coordination and some loss of organizational effectiveness.

PUBLIC STRATEGY

As a business operates, its decisions will have a social impact that will make some ongoing dialog necessary with various elements in society. From time to time a business will need approval from a government or other element of society or it may wish to influence legislation or in other ways to induce society to provide assistance.

The strategic element is management's decision on the form and posture through which necessary dialog with society will be conducted. Some firms take a humble, passive role in such matters by relying largely on the administrative structure of the regulatory bodies, complying with requests, and accepting the rulings that result. Other firms approach these relationships with a stronger posture, attempting positively to expedite the process and influence the outcome. Still others will dispute an outcome that does not please them, as the textile industry has sought protection against imports, by carrying the issue into political and public discussion and attempting to stir support that will resolve any issue in their favor.

Public discussion and public issues are uncomfortable for some firms; they may try to get their public business done as quietly as possible. Other businesses may want a strong public presence as a part of their overall pattern of operations and may seek it in a relatively issue-free manner, as Du Pont did by image advertising and public relations activity aimed at broad, favorable exposure of the enterprise name. Still others plunge directly into issues, as Mobil did in the post-OPEC embargo years, establishing a new and independent public image by putting forward its opinions on public issues related to its business.

A wide range of options is available to any enterprise and to the individual businesses within an enterprise. The strategic choice is the selection of an option compatible with the needs and desires of the firm and with the time and talents of those who must implement it, plus a routine pattern for this interaction with society so that the organization as a whole can play the desired role. Creation of a specialized public relations or public affairs function is common; sometimes it includes the community relations function and sometimes not. Frequently separate staffs charged with specific regulatory relationships are created to handle its extensive dealings with a particular agency, for example, the Food and Drug Administration. The general counsel sometimes oversees necessary interaction with legislative bodies and government officials or a separate organizational unit may be charged with all lobbying and related activities.

According to the functions that management wants performed as part of its public strategy, a corresponding organization structure will be created. The rest of the organization needs to know how it relates to this structure and what its own role should be. More and more often now some unexpected public issue puts a minor manager in the position of having to speak for the enterprise, and that manager needs advance guidance.

OPERATIONS

Each of the major functions of management—planning, organizing, staffing, directing, and controlling—has its component elements and procedures, as has the management operating system itself. Each of these procedures should be considered for its potential vulnerability to outside events.

A useful comparison is with parallel procedures and processes elsewhere, plus the potential application of new technology from any source. The vulnerability is to events in the flow of social, political, and technological change in which the organization and its external environment are immersed.

The plan that is needed for management of corporate operations should adapt the operation to any impact from these external processes. By doing so it continually redirects the inertia of the organization as it rolls forward into the future, shifting direction and emphasis in the way most appropriate to keep the firm's operations current, effective, productive, and competitive.

Productive and Service Units

One major distinction between operating units is based on their functional differences; some have a productive purpose and others provide a service. Units with a productive purpose exist to make or process something; the need for the unit and the evaluation of its performance can be based on the quantity, quality, and cost of the output. Service units function in support of the productive efforts; therefore the demand for their services is a derived demand. The evaluation of their output is also derived from their contribution to the functioning of the productive units.

Production, distribution, and sales are productive functions, in each case with a tangible output of units produced, orders handled, or sales achieved. All three depend on personnel services, but personnel can measure only derived contributions. Even though employee turnover ratios and staff cost per employee may be calculated, it can never be entirely clear how much the personnel function contributes to overall profits.

Maintenance has a similar service role. Individual maintenance tasks can be measured against engineered performance standards, but the intangibles of the manner in which the service benefits the output from the productive units have much more to do with the real contribution of maintenance to the operating whole. Even research is justified by productive output of new products, even though time lags may be long and measurement difficult. Most corporate staffs are service units and have little tangible output. They can be measured only by estimating their contribution to making the total enterprise function effectively.

Whether a unit is primarily of a productive or service nature may not be determined by its location in the organization. Inside an administrative staff division a printing and duplicating function may be a productive unit in cost, delivery, and quality competition with outside vendors. Yet the scheduling office of a major production unit often has no performance measures other than its service in providing workable schedules.

The importance of the distinction between productive and service functions is in the management process as the managers respond to performance measures. Productive processes are measured by their ability to generate a profit or a profit contribution. Service processes are measured by comparing their costs with the benefits perceived by the rest of the organization. The management tasks of the two types of unit are almost exactly parallel. The difference is in the way that the management control process affects the behavior of the managers in charge of particular units.

A productive unit justifies resource requests by its ability to produce more or to produce for less. It can get more resources than it really needs if the results are favorable, but may be denied even critical priorities when the bottom line looks bad. A service unit must deal entirely with management perception of benefits from its services compared with their cost. Because of the intangible nature of the benefits, the process inevitably becomes somewhat subjective and political.

The management processes of the two different types of unit must be focused on achieving two fundamentally different objectives. One is a bottom-line output measure and the other, a politically acceptable cost/benefit ratio. This difference is pervasive and effects the whole psychology of management. The management process gears itself for a political/budgetary control in the case of the service processes versus a market/economic control for the productive processes.

An organization focused on service must emphasize the benefit/cost ratio of these services and promote it as effectively as possible to keep the constituency supporting the services convinced that these benefits far exceed their cost. The response desired from this constituency is one of belief and perception. The arguments are generally framed on subjective gounds and presented or lobbied in a way that will have the greatest impact on these beliefs.

By contrast, an organization whose primary purpose is productive has a bottom-line measure from which it is difficult to escape. Its internal processes orient around the revenues that will be generated, the profits that will be received, and the best way to present and defend them.

Structure and Work Planning

The performance of the business process is carried out in a large number of routine operations which deal with the combination of current requirements and accustomed habit patterns. These habit patterns are a part of building a sound, productive routine. As such, they become central to the operation and must be respected.

One key element in work planning for any group at any level in the organization is the choice of what will be fixed and what variable. Most managements work out a pattern of things that are usually the same—these are the elements of the routine procedures—and design this pattern to accommodate the variable elements as they most frequently occur. The human personality has keyed into it a certain requirement for structure and a certain resistance to change. Both traits were survival requirements for the primitive tribes from which human civilization later developed. In a modern organization the same traits are still important factors that govern behavior.

An automobile assembly plant developed a smooth, repetitive procedure for painting automobile wheels: the operator purged the spray gun, reconnected a paint hose, sprayed four wheels, purged the spray gun again, reconnected a paint hose, and repeated the procedure. The procedure design, with a built-in clean-out and reconnection after each four wheels, meant that the operator could change color for each car by connecting a different hose without varying the preset routine. Because color was designed into this procedure as a variable, the possibility of a change in color with every car had been built into the routine procedure.

In the same way that an automotive engineer planned the wheel-painting routine almost every white-collar or blue-collar job has elements in which change is automatic and accepted and others that seem always to stay the same. A shipping room has a fixed-order picking, packing, and handling routine but bases it on the assumption that no two orders will be the same; each can be shipped to a different address because this flexibility is built into the standard procedure.

Keeping the Structure Flexible

Operating management always has a set of routine procedures with built-in variables; for example, the address was left as a variable in the shipping room routine. Changes in these variables are assumed to be part of the operation. Changes in the procedures themselves must be made with care and planning because the procedures become a part of the familiar structure that the group clings to and protects.

To build a high-performing operation in a changing field it becomes important to structure the routine around those elements likely to change but little and allow rapid or even radical change in the other elements without disturbing the routine. Because the routine procedures were built on changes in packing and addressing, the shipping room could easily ship to the moon—just one more kind of packing material and one more address.

Operating management also has its familiar procedures to which it clings. Within the normal concentration barriers of operating management, reasons for changes in management's own familiar procedures almost never assert themselves. This is why a strategic overview is so essential here to ensure that operations will not lose relevance for lack of changes in management's own process as new factors emerge.

Functional Strategies

The concept of support strategy, introduced in Chapter 2, was of the strategy governing the operating plans and action of a department, function, or other organizational unit. Functional strategies direct the way in which a specific organizational function will be performed—as a subordinate element that contributes to the performance of one or several product, business, and enterprise strategies.

Yet the subordinate position of a functional strategy does not reduce its importance, for it may provide the cutting edge, in terms of leverage, position, or another element, that gives a product, business, or enterprise strategy its potential for success. Many of the best primary strategies are built on the synergism between unusually effective functional strategies in different areas—as a successful and aggressive marketing strategy might be supported by a production strategy that yields an unassailable cost position. Each functional area is itself a separate major area of study and is treated here only briefly to relate it to the various components of the strategic management sequence.

Marketing strategy determines the focus, defines and conveys the leverages, arranges the display, and strives to make best use of available positions and resources. It also attempts to build enduring positions in the marketplace that will yield rent in the future and to establish effective distribution to help selling and as a source of an ongoing distribution service fee. This increases protection against competition and adds to the total that can be reported as profit.

Research and development strategy is designed to guide an effort that is the source of potential new products or services and the vehicle by which the businesses it serves keep their desired relationship to new technology and participate in its application.

The production strategy accomplishes the desired output of goods or services, whether by emphasizing economics of scale, the learning curve, and continuing productivity increases for a basic manufacturer or by extensive subcontracting in a business less concerned about building a proprietary long-term manufacturing position. Hayes and Wheelwright presented a good synthesis of the way in which an effective production strategy can provide the key to an effective overall business strategy.[3]

Distribution, grouped here with marketing, often is organized as a separate function. Engineering, finance, purchasing, personnel, and each of the other specific functional units will have a functional strategy. The importance of specific functions varies greatly from one business to another, but the key is that each function will work toward an effective performance, which includes effective support to the primary strategies.

SUMMARY: MANAGING OPERATIONS

From a strategic overview, management can establish that all procedures are open to change, that reevaluation is constant and ongoing, perhaps that organization members can participate in planning the changes affecting them directly, that the threat to individual employees from change will be moderated by wise management action, but that the organizational norm is one of active preparation for moving into the future.

To plan the management of enterprise operations and to accomplish the dynamic management pattern suggested above, the services of the foresight function discussed earlier are again invaluable. Someone must track events in the outside world by making the bridge to establish relevance when it exists and calling the event or trend to the attention of the operating managers concerned with this component of strategic overview planning. Operating management could do its own environmental search but usually does not, for lack of time in the face of the normal operating pressures. The key is to gather the information for operating management to use to make a plan and act on it, with the key linkages shown in Figure 14.1.

By building toward a more effective and efficient pattern of operation the firm strengthens all present and potential positions

---

[3]Robert H. Hayes and Steven C. Wheelwright, *Restoring Our Competitive Edge: Competition Through Manufacturing* (New York: Wiley, 1984).

based on costs, delivery, and service, thus reinforcing many of its needs-leverages linkages and adding force to the strategies these leverages drive. Thus the basic strength and effectiveness of the operation is a key strategy and action component, as summarized in Figure 14.2.

Organizing the enterprise

Public strategy

Operations

       Productive versus service units
       Structure
       Work planning
       Keeping the structure flexible
       Functional strategies

EXECUTING STRATEGY AND BUILDING PROFITS,
DAY BY DAY

Figure 14.1.   Operations, day by day.

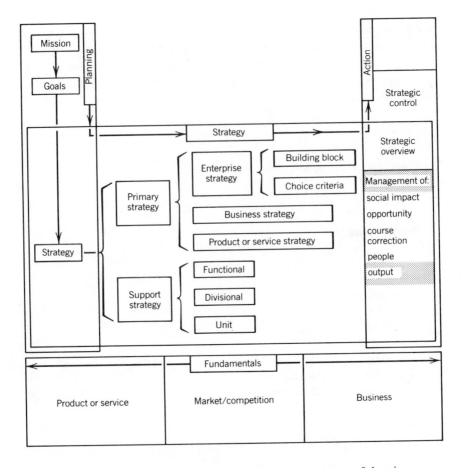

Figure 14.2. Management of operations as key to successful action.

$\equiv$15

KEEPING THE ORGANIZATION VITAL AND EFFECTIVE

Self-renewal is the process by which an organization stays young and vigorous, as it must if it is to continue to design and execute effective strategies. To manage this task the executive group must understand the scope and nature of the self-renewal need and plan for its accomplishment, as discussed in this chapter.

THE RISK OF ORGANIZATIONAL ATROPHY

Organizational self-renewal is the process by which an organization maintains its vitality and effectiveness beyond the tenure of its human components to a theoretically infinite life span. Just as a given molecule of the body is rebuilt with new materials by a continual exchange of chemical entities so the human elements of an organization change with the hiring, firing, promotions, retirements, resignations, and all of the other reasons why one person may replace another in a job.

In spite of the biochemical interchange process, people go through a life cycle. This process is not sufficient to keep all elements of every molecule renewed. The total biological structure matures, ages, and ultimately dies.

Unfortunately, and in spite of the replacement of its human components, an organization ages in almost the same way. The organizational self-renewal task is that of recognizing the ways in which an organization can age, in that its elements become less relevant and less effective, and in overcoming this aging process.

An organization ages in part by formalization, as the connective procedures become overrigid. It ages also in problem solving. As problems recur and become familiar they can be fitted into categories with a solution for each, and as the categories become known and accepted problem solving becomes more and more routine and less cerebral.

This routinization is satisfactory as long as the nature of the problems does not change, but over time the nature of problems always does. One risk of organizational aging is the tendency to continue to use a preplanned set of problem solutions after they have ceased to fit the problems.

OPEN-SYSTEM REQUIREMENTS FOR ORGANIZATIONAL VITALITY

An organization and its management operating system together form a complex open system, with all of the normal open-system characteristics,[1] one of which is the requirement for energy input from outside the system boundaries to prevent function and performance from degrading.

[1] Daniel Katz and Robert L. Kahn, *The Social Psychology of Organizations* (New York: Wiley, 1966), Chapter 2.

This energy-input requirement is the management intervention necessary to keep the system functioning at peak efficiency against changing requirements. A well-run enterprise rarely has major reorganizations because it does not need them. It does not need them because the necessity for organizational change never accumulates. Management is continually making small adjustments in response to need. Over a period of time significant shifts in structure or in personnel are accomplished quietly and almost unnoticed.

This requires a steady input of management energy from outside the open system; that is, from outside the routine components of the operation. When a management gains a strategic overview it attains a position outside the operating routine from which such adjustments can be made.

COMPETENT MANAGERS AND INCOMPETENT SYSTEMS

One of the characteristics of an operating manager who lacks a strategic overview is the way in which this manager becomes embedded in the management operating system and subject to its requirements.

A competent manager will attempt to manage all controllable job elements in an optimum manner. However, evolution of the individual efforts that make up the management operating system must be coordinated if the optimization efforts of individuals are to build toward an optimum for the entire system. But the management operating system, as a system, normally is not managed at all; it grows spontaneously and its function is no one manager's responsibility because it links between managers, primarily at a level of detail beyond the view of the chief executive.

The linkages from manager to manager may get attention in a few areas like materials flow, in which some organizations have a separate system of coordinators or expediters, but with the total management operating system of linkages effectively unmanaged these local efforts will at best represent expedient solutions rather than optimum performance.

If unmanaged, the management operating system degrades spontaneously with time (see Chapter 13). As it degrades, its linkages become less effective and its guidance to individual managers less appropriate. Inside the system operating managers who lack an overview are not able to see this. With the passage of time these managers become more and more competent as they gain experience and the system that links them becomes less and less competent as it loses relevance to the environment for which it was designed. The end point is an incompetent organization staffed with highly competent managers, all strategically blind and unable to understand why their hard work yields so little.

An outside observer may ask how intelligent managers can act the way they do; the answer is that they act intelligently and competently on the basis of the information they have but are controlled by an incompetent system. Operations drift on in this way, slowly degrading, until some final competitive thrust or shift in the environment ends a pitiful status quo. Control changes, heads roll and if the organization survives, it is in a vastly changed form.

THE MANAGEMENT OF ORGANIZATIONAL SELF-RENEWAL

The people at the upper levels of the line and in key staff assignments directly determine the future of the enterprise as the business evolves. They also indirectly determine that future with hiring decisions and by designing business systems and procedures. With the same decision makers governing both processes, failures in perceptions often result in compounded errors. If a missed variable unexpectedly disrupts current programs, it is likely to make demands for managerial knowledge and experience that the firm has also failed to acquire.

The onset of heavy financial penalties for equal employment opportunity compliance failures caught some companies by surprise, even though the requirement was not new and compliance pressure had been building. These companies were forced into the immediate creation of a significant, acceptable program in an area in which none of the management group knew the requirements of the law, how a program should be designed, or how to manage it without disrupting relations with existing employees. Strategic blindness, in not perceiving that this was a new law that had to be obeyed, caused these companies to pay severe penalties for past behavior and to disrupt their current operations in a disorderly attempt at instant compliance. They had defaulted in timely consideration of this problem and in failing to gather the competence to deal with it before it became a crisis.

The largest difficulty in managing needed change in the organization and in the management operating system is in the area in which top management itself is the judge of the need for change and the factor in the system being evaluated. It is hard for members of a top management group to be objective about the efficiency and effectiveness of their own functioning or about future requirements that could call for experience and knowledge they do not possess.

In some cases the only way in which management can accomplish a sufficiently detached strategic overview for an adequate self-renewal plan is by delegating this analysis to an outside committee. Sometimes members of the board of directors have sufficient knowledge and detachment from the operating routine to carry out this portion of the planning. In other cases it is necessary to turn to outside professionals.

In any case, this is a task whose delegation must be handled with care in spite of the urgency of getting the job done well. No management will be comfortable in creating a review committee to make self-renewal recommendations that involve its own future; it will wish to keep control over the committee. Yet the professionals with this assignment will not feel comfortable in making forthright recommendations that could be adverse to some of the managers who will judge the report and authorize payment for it. The most viable compromise can be the supervision of a self-renewal evaluation by a committee of the board of directors, preferably one strong enough to guide the task and sufficiently removed from routine operations to judge them objectively.

ORGANIZATION CULTURE

Organization culture has become an issue and a challenge, particularly since books like *The Art of Japanese Management, In Search of Excellence,* and *Theory Z*[2] have pointed out the potential strategic differences between competitors due to differences in the cultures of their organizations. In the nomenclature used here organization culture is a certain sort of position built by the cumulative impact of the governing strategies on the organization. The way the management operating system accumulates and repeats practices is a basic culture-building process, and the various impacts of the governing strategies are captured in the same way.

American Spirit

One recent analysis of organization culture was Miller's *American Spirit*.[3] After restating the need for changes to restore U.S. industrial strength he built on themes from *In Search of Excellence* and from his own experience to propose a list of eight necessary attributes for a new and competitive American corporate culture:

1. *The Purpose Principle.* *The distinction between the leader and the manager can be summarized by the word "purpose." Leaders have a noble vision of their purpose. Leaders create energy by instilling purpose in others.*

2. *The Excellence Principle.* *Excellence is not an accomplishment. It is a spirit that dominates the life and soul of a person or a corporation. It is the never-ending process of learning that provides its own satisfaction.*

3. *The Consensus Principle.* *The successful manager of the future will make full use of the collective wisdom of those within his jurisdiction and he will learn to derive pleasure, not from the making of decisions, but from assuring that the best possible decision is made.*

4. *The Unity Principle.* *The workers no longer want to be separated*

---

[2]William G. Ouchi, *Theory Z: How American Business Can Meet the Japanese Challenge* (Cambridge, Mass.: Addison-Wesley, 1981).

[3]Lawrence M. Miller, *American Spirit: Visions of a New Corporate Culture* (New York: Morrow, 1984).

from responsibility. They want to participate in the business game and they want to play to win. Let's make them all managers, now!

5. **The Performance Principle.** *The primary law of human behavior is that behavior is a function of its consequences. That which is rewarded increases. When we learn to reward performance we will have performance.*

6. **The Empiricism Principle.** *The primary task of the manager is to think. The future success of the corporation is dependent on his ability to think clearly, critically, and creatively.*

7. **The Intimacy Principle.** *Intimacy is the thread between the inner person, his manager, and the organization they serve. It is intimacy that permits trust, sacrifice, and loyalty.*

8. **The Integrity Principle.** *Leadership requires followership and following is an act of trust, faith in the course of the leader, and that faith can be generated only if the leaders act with integrity.*

Miller's eight attributes sum to a specific picture of internal organizational processes. For the reasoning that led him to these conclusions, *The Art of Japanese Management, In Search of Excellence,* and his *American Spirit* make an excellent trilogy, but, whether Miller's picture is the ultimate or only a proximate description, he proposes a condition very different from the operating pattern in many firms. He then devotes the second half of his book to change processes by which, with careful management, the culture of an organization could be shifted in the direction he recommends.

Reinforcement for Miller's thesis comes from Pascarella's *The New Achievers,*[4] a somewhat parallel study of the way that, given the opportunity to participate and share in the goals, the organization will come alive, unify around its purpose, and rise to new levels of achievement.

Davis addressed this same area in *Managing Corporate Culture.*[5] After developing the importance of corporate culture in determining whether a given business strategy can be carried out, he lays out the necessary change processes. These parallel the organiza-

---

[4]Perry Pascarella, *The New Achievers* (New York: Free Press, 1984).
[5]Stanley M. Davis, *Managing Corporate Culture* (Cambridge, Mass.: Ballinger/Harper & Row, 1984).

tional change processes Miller outlined, except that Davis comes to grips with the way strategies are paralyzed by an inappropriate corporate culture. Davis found cultural obstructions to strategy that this book would attribute to problems with the building block and choice strategies, and then persuaded management to exert the effort necessary to remove these obstructions so that business strategies could operate.

Change and AT&T

No organizational change processes are easy and orderly changes in organization culture are among the more difficult. This point needs reemphasis. A position, whether of a brand name in a marketplace or one represented by organization culture, is built piece by piece over time; in a large organization building the organization culture is like building a glacier. Its inertia is almost as great when there is need to change it in an orderly way, but, unlike a glacier, the culture of an organization is built on basic beliefs and trusts, and it can be shattered like glass if inappropriate management action destroys these basics.

It will be some time before the organizational dynamics of the breakup of the Bell system are fully recognized and analyzed. It is already clear that the basic strategic concepts of AT&T management in proposing the breakup were good, but the system has experienced culture shock and some difficulty in functioning as a federation of independent companies. Pessimists who predict that AT&T will not do well in the next few years do so largely on the basis of arguments translating to a belief that AT&T cannot change its organizational culture fast enough to make its new strategy work.

Like AT&T many other managements will have to change their organization's culture to permit strategies their survival requires, and such changes must be managed skillfully if they are to yield a better outcome rather than a worse.

Logical Incrementalism

In addition to the organizational mechanisms of cultural change, there are other important dimensions. James Brian Quinn's

Strategies for Change[6] made an excellent case for an incremental approach to change in large organizations; that is, instead of mapping out all of the steps in some global shift management should decide on the direction and take the first small step. Another step should follow, and another, until ultimately the change is accomplished. The advantages are twofold: (1) the small steps do not create an undue threat to anyone and the organization has time for orderly adaptation, and (2) each step is planned from the present at the time that it is taken; thus the variations between expectation and achievement are accommodated, and the inevitable zigzagging as other pressures fall on the organization does not prevent a reasonably straight ultimate course to the objective.

Quinn's contribution is his realistic approach to the dynamics of change in large organizations. He does not build from the same organizational change background as Miller, Pascarella, and Davis, and his analysis provides a powerful insight into the change process.

The Organizational Change Matrix

Leontiades analyzed organizational growth and change processes and developed a useful matrix (Figure 15.1) that contrasts a steady-state and an evolutionary management style as a firm moves up or down the scale from a **single business** to a **dominant single business** to a **multibusiness** with **related** or **unrelated** activities.[7] The management problems and organizational requirements change significantly as the firm moves from one box to another or attempts to move, fails to accomplish the necessary changes, and falls back. From this matrix and from other dimensions of the shifts in requirements for structure, planning, and management Leontiades provides another series of insights into the nature of the organizational transitions that successful strategy changes require.

---

[6]James Brian Quinn, *Strategies for Change: Logical Incrementalism* (Homewood, Ill.: Richard D. Irwin, 1980).
[7]Milton Leontiades, *Strategies for Diversification and Change* (Boston: Little, Brown, 1980).

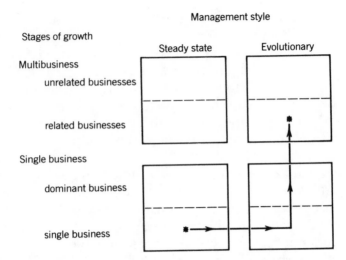

Figure 15.1. Leontiades organizational change matrix.*

Culture Summary

Organization culture is important and requires careful management in times of change, but it is a dependent variable. To
reemphasize: organizational culture is a dependent variable. Some
of the great entrepreneurs of the past would undoubtedly argue
that, given a top management with sufficient integrity, respect for
the individual, clear, shared goals based on real customer needs,
and firmness of purpose, the culture would take care of itself.

SOCIETY'S NEED FOR BUSINESS SELF-RENEWAL

The corporation as a legal form through which business is
accomplished is essentially eternal. It need never cease to function
if its parts are kept up to date, well integrated with one another and
with the customers, suppliers, and others on which the business
depends.

Not only is the business corporation theoretically capable of
eternal life, but the enterprise assumes a role in society that should

*From Milton Leontiades, *Strategies for Diversification and Change,* p. 74. Copyright © 1980
by Milton Leontiades. Reprinted by permission of Little, Brown and Company (Inc.).

require it to function indefinitely. The social responsibility elements that require management of social impact mostly require a business with an eternal life.

The community depends on the business—not only this year and next year but forever. The employees depend on the business for continued employment; although individually they will age and retire, others will take their places, and the dependency will go on, forever or until the business defaults on maintenance of the expected ties. The same is true of customer expectations for a continued supply of their favorite products and of supplier expectations that the firm will continue to buy the products that were tailored to fit its needs. Society needs and hopes for business firms that will last forever.

The stockholders and managers have an even larger stake in a continuing business. The means to long business life is through careful planning, by constructing a plan for organizational self-renewal, and then putting this plan into action, not as a one-time exercise but as a steady, gentle paring and reshaping to keep the organization and the management operating system current, lean, and effective.

SUMMARY: STRUCTURE FOLLOWS STRATEGY

When Chandler wrote that structure follows strategy he was referring to the way that major changes in enterprise strategy at Du Pont, General Motors, and Standard Oil required complete redesign of the organizational structure. The same principle applies in this area of organizational self-renewal.

If the management strategy does not include management of the management operating system the organization will degrade slowly in routine performance of the policies set down when the governing strategies were last thoroughly examined. Because policies usually require modification at least in details as external circumstances change, the organization sometimes drifts away from its chosen strategy as policy details age. If the operating details of the action and consequences flowing from a given strategy are not reexamined and modified as necessary, they will not trigger necessary changes in the organization structure.

A good organization changes almost continually as management adapts to changes in requirements and cataclysmic reorganization is rarely required. The organization also needs a plan and strategy to deal with the self-renewal problem (Figure 15.2) to allow its structure to evolve as its strategy shifts. Then, because the overall evaluation and evolution process keep the strategy and structure vital and effective, the operating managers will be effectively linked. Their individual competence adds up to an effective system more likely to prosper and survive. The strategies dependent on their efforts are more likely to be correctly executed and more effective in the marketplace, thus making this self-renewal management area another key strategy and action component (Figure 15.3).

The risk of organizational atrophy

Open-system requirements for organizational vitality

Competent managers and incompetent systems

The management of organizational self-renewal

Organization culture

    American Spirit
    Change and AT&T
    Logical incrementalism
    The organizational change matrix

Society's need for business self-renewal

STRUCTURE CHANGES WITH STRATEGY TO KEEP THE
BUSINESS ALIVE

Figure 15.2. Self-renewal as a survival requirement.

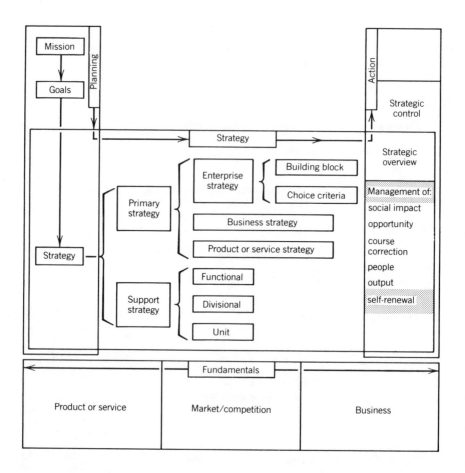

Figure 15.3. Self-renewal management as key to continued successful action.

This chapter completes Part 4, which has reviewed the components of enterprise strategy and the organization as a part of the process for designing effective strategies. These are key components because their level of performance is a strategy-design constraint in the present and because new needs often require changes in these components for continued effectiveness in the future.

PART 5

Practicing Strategic Management

☰16

EFFECTIVE
STRATEGIES

In the flow from planning to strategy to action, the action step yields the results that justify the sequence and continue the profitable evolution of the organization. The final key component, therefore, is the strategic management process in which the correct action is taken (Figure 16.1). The final section of this book deals with this strategic management as it relates to the strategy and action components laid out earlier and then in a final summary.

A strategy is an abstraction. By itself it cannot make profits. Only specific actions can lead to profits. A good strategy must lead to action, and the actions it specifies must be actions that the organization can carry out successfully. Therefore the action-ability of the organization is often a key strategy constraint and is emphasized here.

225

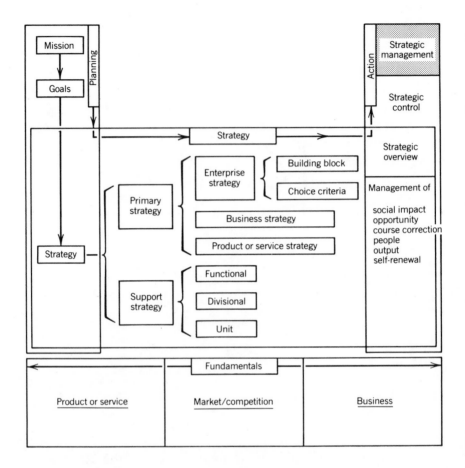

Figure 16.1. The role of strategic management

This book began with basics such as making up rules and creating resources and the essential linkage from mission to goals to strategy and action. Then it outlined the underlying product, market, and business characteristics and began to draw these separate ideas together into a process for designing strategy.

Defining the role of the governing strategies also led to the excellence model as a realizable ultimate in organizational effectiveness, to the boundaries problem, from the governing strategies and from organizational barriers, and to needs-leverages linkages as central to effective strategies and their design. Strategic blindness, which can be disastrous, can be avoided by a strategic overview. These ideas, with effective strategic control, can lead to a process for designing and executing winning strategies.

A winning strategy must be effective. This chapter discusses the efficiency and effectiveness of strategies and the importance of having good rent collectors, plus more on creating resources and finding power for a strategy.

MEASURING EFFECTIVENESS

The need and the challenge in designing strategies is to plan the right actions and execute them. The necessary standard of performance is set by customers and competition; a strategy resulting in a product or service that is more effective in meeting customer needs than its alternatives is likely to be successful. Thus Goliath rose among the Philistines and became their champion. For a long time his individual combat strategy was highly successful—until he met David. Like Goliath, many on-going strategies could be defeated, but they stand as adequate until some David mounts a successful challenge.

Many analysts have commented on the change in the computer market in the last several years. Clearly it was much easier to compete successfully when IBM was preoccupied with the antitrust suit. Now it requires a much better strategy to make headway.

The point is to underscore the difference between effectiveness and efficiency. Successful strategy starts by being effective; it is necessary to focus on the real needs of customers and to satisfy them. It also helps to understand the dimensions of these needs, as Henry Ford apparently sensed the price elasticity of the car market. The first cars were toys of the affluent and few could afford them, but as Ford created assembly line production, achieved scale economies, and moved down a learning curve he cut the price profitably to such a level that the mass market opened.

When a strategy is effective in meeting customer needs, it

returns a profit to the producer, who would otherwise go out of business. However, many successful strategies are not efficiently executed and at the time it may matter very little. If sales and profits are good and growing, who cares?

Then, when competition moves in, the situation changes. A strategy is no longer effective if it ceases to yield a profit. Businesses not able to regain effectiveness disappear rapidly. It has been suggested that the problem confronting much of U.S. basic industry is that life was so easy for 25 or more years after World War II that competition was largely between unimaginative domestic producers and that whole industries were able to generate steady profits without any real need for competitive efficiency, to the point that now the industrial base must be rebuilt to reestablish U.S. competitive parity.

In any case, the requirement of strategy design in the short term is for a strategy that yields a profit, whether or not the resulting operation is efficient. In the longer term good management demands at least a competitive level of efficiency, and excellent management demands excellence in terms of the best current operation and a steady rate of improvement. Against an excellence standard, strategy design becomes more demanding, more effective, and more likely to generate long-term sales and profits.

Strategy design is governed by a series of enterprise-level decisions regarding the kind of enterprise the firm chooses to be, the kind of operation it will engage in, and the risks it will accept. For any firm in a demanding environment performance according to the excellence model may be required, and this is achievable only under good management with the proper people and leadership strategies.

To formulate sound product and business strategy within the boundaries of the firm the organization must permit personal and responsible strategy design and execution, with accountability of the key managers, whether by use of strategic business units or in some other way.

Business strategy and product or service strategy are based on needs-leverages linkages, and as the requirements for establishing these linkages are explored the innovation, cost cutting, market-positioning, and promotion potentials can be explored.

IS YOUR STRATEGY GOOD ENOUGH?

An effective strategy is one that is better, in terms of needs-leverages linkages, at fulfilling a specific role in the marketplace than any competitive strategy. There is no theoretical or practical limit to the amount that the competitive strategies can be improved because each is based on the ingenuity of a more or less hungry management in devising new approaches and new rules for the competitive game to gain a larger share. The history of competition is that any strategy sooner or later loses effectiveness because others find a way to narrow its advantage and then surpass it. Patents expire or can be bypassed, know-how diffuses across an industry, and even the best technology or process ceases to be the best as innovation continues.

For a given firm to seize the lead and keep it, it must start with an effective strategy; that is, one sufficiently better in relation to its market targets so that it can win a profitable share. It must then improve its position until its leadership is established. This strategy must be based on superior leverages to succeed. Most good leverages can be made into enduring positions. Market leadership itself is a position, and the scale economies and learning-curve potential of the market leader can usually be made into cost and distribution positions.

The market leader should be able to accumulate positions that reinforce its initial strategy. This makes maintenance of that strategy easier and the leadership more profitable. It is a little like the old king-of-the-hill game in which, everything else being equal, the child on the hilltop had the advantage and could stay there. This means that the market leader often can hold market share with little effort. Reinforced by the leader's various positions, products or services may not need to be as good as the competitors' and success continues.

The differential between the established leader and its competition is based on a relatively fixed level of rent earned by the positions of the leaders and any inferiority in the leader's products or services uses up a part of that differential. This often means that the margin between the leading and a competitive strategy narrows over time. Then a competitor devises a new approach, an innovation that in some way increases the effectiveness of its strategy even temporarily, and draws ahead of the leader. The leader meanwhile has become dependent on rent from positions based on leadership that melt away as its leadership fails. Either the leader mounts a successful counterattack or, more often, leadership shifts and the former leader fades away.

The alternative, more difficult, but more effective role for a firm that has won to leadership is to continue a steady and unrelenting effort to improve its products, leverages, and positions. This has four internal justifications:

1. Many product or service markets have significant price elasticity; better operations mean lower costs, and if the leader can afford to cut prices the market may grow and profit increase.
2. It helps profits a lot to keep improving the costs.
3. "Someone else will do it if we don't—just keep making things better."
4. "If someone is trying to gain on us it sure will give them fits when we cut the price."

This is the excellence model again, of course. Create a good operation based on an effective strategy and keep every person sincerely involved in making the products, operations, and customer services better every day.

SUBSTANCE GOVERNS STRATEGY

The need and challenge in designing strategy is to plan the right actions and execute them. This requires the uncommon ability to examine business situations and to see the substance through the forms.

The manager of an American Cyanamid feed-blending department noticed that quantities of export orders from his plant were being returned unsold for salvage or reprocessing, sometimes a year or two later. Export shipments went to a warehouse to be held until export clearances, import licenses, and letters of credit could be obtained. This took many months, with order changes and cancellations. Packages became dirty in the warehouse and bags got broken. The products, which had a limited shelf life, sometimes reached the point at which not enough of their dating remained for them to be sold.

The department head asked why the products had to be produced before the clearance to ship them had been obtained. At first no one could answer the question; then someone realized that the product lot numbers were needed for processing the clearance papers. The department head then suggested that the lot numbers be assigned and that his crew print the bags for the product; these bags would be held empty in his plant until a few days before shipping and then filled with the appropriate product.

This proposal caused much confusion and met a great deal of resistance because it was so unorthodox, but no one could find anything wrong with it. The department head kept insisting on an answer and finally his idea was tried. It worked well. A large in-process inventory disappeared, to the point that Cyanamid discovered it no longer needed a major warehouse in Fairlawn, New Jersey. The total savings, which included avoided loss of dated products, reduced inventory carrying charges, and handling and warehousing, were never made known because the change was so simple that it embarrassed a number of managers.

After this change had been absorbed by the system and some of those responsible had reflected on it the embarrassment increased, for it was realized that it was not necessary to preprint the product packages for the export shipments; lot numbers were easy to preassign and reserve; this permitted all paperwork to go forward, and the production could then be scheduled a few days before the desired shipping date. When this change was made the system had finally moved to the point at which it should have STARTED if any one of the dozens of analysts and managers involved in its function had thought about the substance of the export order processing rather than the forms and procedures.

The point is not to single out Cyanamid but to suggest that a common failing in organizations, particularly large ones, is for people to do their jobs in terms of procedures and instructions without thinking at all about the task. Effective strategy must be based on the substance of the process, and it is unlikely to be formulated by a manager who has not trained him- or herself to look past the procedures and come to grips with the substance.

THE ENTREPRENEUR AS A RENT COLLECTOR

Positions are a key element of business and product strategies, as discussed earlier. Their value is something to build on, a resource that makes possible leverages to increase the effectiveness of a strategy. As such, positions earn a return in the marketplace in the form of rent, as discussed in Chapter 4.

The rent a position earns is its contribution to the profitability of a strategy. That profit potentially has many sources; for example, effective distribution service could be one and brokerage between bulk purchases and smaller sales, another. The two most variable sources of profit for a strategy are innovation and rent, the largest and most exciting when you have them but they can fade away to zero; a distribution or a brokerage profit will normally be more constant. Profits from innovation are the returns to the creation of a product or service with superior needs-leverages linkages, something better people will willingly pay more for or something equally good for less money, but the impact of the innovation is clear-cut and its profits are often generous.

Rent is less obvious but perhaps equally important over the long term. A patent, by definition a monopoly, earns rent to the extent of its profit contribution if it bars a competitor from the market. To the extent that the Hoffmann-La Roche position in the Valium market was due to a now-expired patent on this drug substance, that patent earned handsome rents. Actually many other positions contribute, and probably the franchise of the product with the medical profession and with consumers has more importance than the patent, but these are also positions that earn rent.

Any position has the potential to help create leverages and earn rent. The manager whose zone of authority includes various positions should count them among the resources managed. That manager's boss should ask what sort of rents each of these positions is earning and what will be done to increase these rent collections. This brings the discussion to the entrepreneur as rent collector because this is an important role. Coca-Cola long resisted any secondary use of its Coke market franchise in spite of a large rent potential, on the basis that it might dilute the position and endanger its ability to continue the long-term Coke profit flows, an important and substantial rent stream. Then, more recently, when changes in competition and taste brought the need for variations on the traditional Coca-Cola product, the Coke brand franchise was broadened successfully to include diet and other new products. Some of the key management decisions at Coca-Cola in recent years, therefore, were those concerned with the Coca-Cola company's rent collections.

Whether the position is a brand name, a superior distribution access to a market, an advantageous production or raw materials position, or mastery of a difficult technology, the strategic question is how to get the most rent. Sometimes this involves broader use of the brand or other position and sometimes it does not, depending on the situation and the likely competitive consequences. However, the success of major market forces—IBM comes to mind—is earned in part because they know how to get maximum rents from their positions and at the same time how to keep strengthening them so that these rents will continue into the future. Some of their top managers and entrepreneurs are very good rent collectors.

FOR THE GOOD OF THE COMPANY

The excellence model requires an intense personal dedication to the good of the company by all members of its organization. To achieve this dedication each member of management works to help each employee become a part of the effort by finding a worthwhile personal purpose within the span of the company interests and then concentrating his or her energies on achieving that purpose.

This involvement is not possible if employees are distracted excessively by personal concerns, and a part of the price of obtaining it is to have the company do what it can to minimize these concerns. The company can provide job security, rewards and personal progress in proportion to performance and ability, and security for the employees' dependents, and the manager can help to make sure that all members of his or her unit are treated fairly by the organizational system.

To repeat: this is not a benefit based on charity. If employees must fight their own battles, this becomes a distraction. By providing a work climate in which employees can depend on their managers and their company for these things the merit of the company cause is increased at the same time that employees are made freer to concentrate on achievement.

This relationship and requirement are sound and work out well for all concerned within an enterprise whose people strategy uniformly reinforces such behavior. In other sorts of organizations the manager falls into an ambiguous situation. The internal dynamics of his or her unit require this managerial role to achieve the enthusiasm and productivity that could bring promotion. Yet the necessary rewards and accommodations from outside the manager's zone of authority may not be available when needed, and the personal dynamics of the group can be wrecked and the manager personally discredited if he or she has seemed to promise what is then not available. A manager's inability to get fair treatment for an employee in some procedural matter or some insensitive company-wide mandate on expenses or employment practices may show up the local manager's concern for the employees as a sham company-wide.

There is no clear resolution of this ambiguous position. The use of the excellence model within that manager's own unit risks implied promises of respect and earned rewards the larger organization may not honor, but not to attempt maximum effectiveness of the individual unit is for the manager to lower personal aspirations for performance and promotions.

NEEDS-LEVERAGES LINKAGES

Needs-leverages linkages are the key. The mission of a business defines its desire to satisfy specific customer needs. Within that mission certain needs are the target of each product, but for an effective strategy to exist the product or service must be linked to these needs: (1) by an ability to satisfy them; (2) by the customer's perception that they can be satisfied in a cost effective manner, and (3) by leverages giving the customer motivation to purchase that product at the required price as a means of satisfaction. All the rest is preliminary and has little meaning until a leverage is created in the customer's perceptions strong enough to cause the purchase.

When many others are competing to satisfy the same need of the same consumer the issue is no different. The consumer learns that many vendors are competing, by some personal process accepts some of them as possible sources of the desired product, selects one, and makes the purchase. The successful vendor has established a better system of needs-leverages linkages in that customer's perception than the unsuccessful competitors, whether by bidding a tenth of a cent lower on the annual corporate requirement for sulfuric acid or by putting a product in a more appealing package. Effective needs-leverage linkages are central; without them the strategy must fail.

The entire key to a sound strategy is that it be built on an effective, fulfillable system of needs-leverages linkages. For long-term success the excellence model demands a steady effort to make those needs-leverages linkages better, year by year, week by week, and day by day.

DESIGN OF ENTERPRISE STRATEGY

The building block strategies and the choice criteria determine the nature and, to an extent, the capabilities of the enterprise, as emphasized several times, but there is no simple recipe for enterprise strategy, because every firm should not be the same and enterprise strategy is designed to develop different enterprises. Some of the characteristics controlled by enterprise strategy are the success requirements of certain businesses; that is, a business based on the development of new high-technology products could hardly prosper in an enterprise with a passive opportunity strategy or a risk-averse payoff strategy. The leadership and people strategies together determine the degree to which these businesses have potential for achieving the effectiveness inherent in the excellence model, where some business situations require this level of effectiveness.

Others among the enterprise strategies are more flexible according to the tastes and ambitions of a given management group. Desirability strategy is directly related to the tightness and intensity of the goal pattern of that firm, managing strategy defines the extent and nature of the diversity added to the management task, and belonging strategy accommodates other organizational preferences and barriers that should influence decisions. For a conglomerate these three set a rather loose pattern focused on financial return and a much tighter and more subjective constraint for an enterprise that concentrates on one or two business areas.

Public strategy is the most independent of the five building blocks, although the market profile set by the impact of the basic businesses tends to set a minimum level. Management may choose to escalate this public role, as Mobil did after the oil embargo or as Manville did by its bankruptcy strategy, or it may choose a quiet role, as American Home Products and Beatrice Foods did for a great many years.

The resource strategy is partly independent of the others but also determined in part by the firm's attitude toward debt financing and the financial community. Resource strategy is also heavily influenced by the outcomes of leadership, people, and opportunity strategies; the excitement and reward of successful resource creation often seems to attract funds to a dynamic business.

Enterprise strategy must accommodate the interests and abilities of the management group that designs and must operate it and the market requirements for effectiveness of the business and product strategies. If the enterprise prospers enterprise, business, and product strategies will be proved adequate. If profits falter often all three levels of strategy must be recast.

MAKING UP RULES AND CREATING RESOURCES

The means to an effective set of needs-leverages linkages is human ingenuity. The business is operated by a group of managers who must make up a workable set of rules for operating it to fulfill the selected needs-leverages linkages in the face of competition. To do this they must obtain resources by buying them or creating them, where the key organizational resources are available only by creation. Human ingenuity is the key to better rules for running the business to increase its competitive advantage, generate better needs-leverages linkages, and devise better plans for creating resources. Good management, plus intelligence thoughtfully and ingeniously applied, is required in the execution. The consequence again is in the pattern of the excellence model and yields good profits and good personal rewards.

THE POWER TRIPOD

Designing strategy is something like the farm-era problem of pulling up a stump or lifting a tractor engine. Given three strong timbers to make a tripod and suitable tackle, almost any large object can be lifted. Given the problem of something heavy to lift, solution starts by finding hoisting tackle powerful enough to lift it—a chain hoist to raise an engine block or a set of good needs-leverages linkages to raise sales in the marketplace. Then there must be a tripod strong enough to take the strain—three good fence posts to pull up a stump and careful support from the characteristics of the product, the market, and the business itself, in a strategy for increasing sales.

Chapters 4, 5, and 6 dealt with the product, market, and business characteristics. Their purpose was to highlight key features in these three areas. Their role in strategy design is to aid in constructing a robust basis for that strategy in each area. The needs-leverages linkages must provide the power to convince the necessary numbers of customers to buy, but their effectiveness depends on sturdy support, thorough understanding of the fundamental characteristics of the product, competition and market, and the business. Just as a farmer who tried to pull up a stump was sometimes hurt when one leg of his tripod broke, the power of the hoist is to no avail without strong supports. Good needs-leverages linkages are essential and sound fundamentals are equally essential. No one wants to have something fail and the strategy come tumbling down.

POWER FOR THE STRATEGY

The strategy tripod requires three strong legs to support it from product, market, and business foundations, plus needs-leverages linkages powerful enough to overcome the resistance. However, the leverages do not work alone. A lever by itself does not raise a weight but it can magnify the force exerted. The potential increase of a force by a suitable system of leverages is enormous. Archimedes said that with a suitable lever he could move the world. The working of any powerful system of leverages depends on the force applied, the nature of the leverages, and the amount of resistance to be overcome.

Needs-leverages linkages tie a product or service to a customer need in a way that is intended to cause the customer to see their value and make the purchase. The power of the lever, to make the purchase actually happen, comes from that customer's perceptions of the need and the ability of that power or service to fill it.

Power for the levers—as a marketer attempts to sharpen the customer's perception of the need, to increase urgency, and reduce the deferability of the purchase, and works even harder to establish the potential for a specific product or service to fill that customer's need better and more favorably than any alternative. There are two sources of power: the pressures of the customer's need and the potency of the product offering, both based on the buyer's perception as reinforced by the seller.

Both sources of power are invoked first by the skill and deftness of the sales effort and more fundamentally by the intrinsic merit of the product that fills the need in a superior way. Creation of this power is by producing an effective deliverable and presenting it well. The first Xerox copiers were so superior to their alternatives for most purposes that the issue was almost entirely one of need, in its degree and urgency. If the customer could be convinced of the need for a copier, the Xerox was almost the only way to fill the need. The power applied to the leverages and the power of the strategy was based on effective programs for spreading the use of copying.

Now many good copy machines are available. The power applied to the leverages for an effective copier marketing strategy is based largely on differential advantages—why one machine is better or less expensive in a certain application than the others. The customer needs are little changed, although with new features and less expensive machines the market continues to expand. The purchase leverages have become comparative and the needs-leverages linkages build on "a better way to satisfy your copying needs."

Some copier strategies are based on technological advances: advanced controls, easier care, and less maintenance. Others emphasize quality, reliability, and service in relation to alternatives. Still others feature the low cost of the machine, of owning it, or of the per-copy cost of its services. This means that various copier manufacturers are competing to produce better copiers technically, machines and copies of higher quality, copiers easier to care for, more reliable, and requiring less service, and lower cost machines or machines lowering the cost per copy. All of these features are demanding to obtain and many organizations are competing for the same advances in each feature.

Various manufacturers have established positions in the copier market—the Xerox position is the most formidable—but none seems to be yielding large rents. The market has adjusted to copier availability from many vendors and other manufacturers have had many years to match the original Xerox cost and manufacturing positions. It seems probable that the successful survivors in this market will be those able to gain comparative advantage over their competitors most rapidly and consistently.

This competition is not over the ability to do a task but to do it better and more rapidly than competitive groups. The outcome therefore should be determined by the relative skills of the several managements in selecting targets and the relative effectiveness of their organizations in achieving them. This is a market in which the excellence model will make a difference. This is a market in which the power applied to the leverages must come primarily from performance of the organization.

With many vendors constructing needs-leverages linkages based on the same set of needs, this is a market in which one or several of the different sorts of organizational effectiveness—in developing new features in quality, reliability, and performance, in cost, in field support of the machines—will determine who combines the most force and the best leverages; that is, who transmits the most force from its leverages to the need and gains the market advantage.

Power for the strategy must be sufficient to drive the needs-leverages linkages if the strategy is to be effective. This means good presentation of good products, of course, and much more if the market is competitive. As competitive pressure rises, the strategy requires better leverages and more power. When established positions no longer yield rents large enough to protect the leader, as they once protected Xerox, the competitive issue will be determined by quality of management and organization and some elements of chance. The more difficult the competitive situation may be, the more carefully constituted the strategy must be, and the more the excellence model will help to make it effective—to make it profitable, that is.

STRATEGY AND THE EXCELLENCE MODEL

Strategy is the means of accomplishing an end. To achieve this end management obtains and uses a wide variety of tools and resources, some purchased and some created. One of the most potent management tools is an excellent organization, a tool of which the creating managers become a part and one of the most valuable resources a management can create.

Not all strategies require excellent or even good organizations to be effective. Some of the high flying new software and computer companies did extremely well for some time with organizations later shown to be weak and disorganized. A strategy needs enough power behind it to be effective. If the leverages are extremely good or the competition weak, less power is required.

Success in strategy design is in having strategies that prove to be effective in use. The science is in putting them together well, with good needs-leverages linkages and sufficient power to drive them. The art is in knowing how much power is really sufficient and the excellent organization always keeps trying to add a little more.

SUMMARY: DESIGNING EFFECTIVE STRATEGIES

Each strategy must be built on sufficiently strong and adequately powered needs-leverages linkages. However, the issues on which a strategy turns are those of substance, not form or appearance; they require that managers have the ability to cut through to the substance. And, often a strategy depends on skill in maintaining and building positions so that the addition of the rent they generate can bring the total return to the desired levels.

Effective strategies frequently depend on the efforts of the people in the organization, efforts that grow out of a relationship the organization needs and can maintain if the design of the enterprise strategies encourage it, as summarized in Figure 16.2.

A strategy is proved effective when it works; that is, the true and final measure is success in execution. There is no theoretical standard for strategies and only the competitive pressures of the marketplace to ensure that the weak strategies will eventually be toppled.

Needs-leverages linkages

The power tripod
Power to the strategy

Substance governs strategies
Build good positions
Be a good rent collector

Making up rules and creating resources

The people of the organization
Control through enterprise strategy
Strategy and the excellence model

GOOD ENOUGH TO YIELD A PROFIT

Figure 16.2.   Effective strategies.

≡17

SUMMARY: FROM PLANNING AND STRATEGY TO ACTION

Successful action means doing the right things at the right times. Effective strategies are those that lead to successful action. What action will succeed at a given time depends on many things, including all circumstances and alternatives and an element of luck. Designing effective strategy, the subject of this book, is the science and art of considering circumstances and alternatives and how to deal with them in order to choose strategies leading to successful action.

Success means that the strategy works; that is, it brings about the desired results. This may be easy or difficult. Most experienced managers can give examples of successful strategies that really should have failed but some fortunate combination of circumstances carried them through. Most can name a corporate Goliath, a vulnerable company that will nonetheless continue to prosper until some David takes note and attacks. Most collections of strategy stories also include good strategies that deserved to succeed but did not for some accidental or unforeseeable reason. The conclusion is that the strategy design process can be fallible, in spite of the best efforts of the participants, because the world of real markets and organizations contains so many surprises, good and bad.

Most strategies do not encounter the radical, unpredictable good or bad fortune that overrides plans and forecasts. Most well-planned strategies can be executed according to these plans and yield approximately the desired results; that is, strategy can be designed, and if the design process discussed in earlier chapters is well executed the action directed by that strategy will be successful in most cases. The purpose of this chapter is to summarize that process.

POLICY, STRATEGY, AND THE BUSINESS FIRM

The action directed by a strategy should be aimed at achieving one or more goals. Preceding the design of a strategy, therefore, should be any necessary clarification of the goal or goals at which it is aimed. These goals exist within the framework of a mission toward which the efforts of the unit are dedicated. Basic as this seems, it is of the utmost importance because of the many cases in which failures in strategy and action trace back to uncertainties in the goal structure or a lack of understanding of the underlying purpose or social role on which the organization's efforts should have been focused. The mission or social role comes first; it allows the definition of a series of goals for management action. The design of strategies to achieve those goals, and the planning and strategy to action sequence stressed here, then follows.

Strategies differ greatly in their characteristics according to their level and their relation to the business or organizational purpose. The basic strategies governing the creation and sale of products or services are constructed (1) of a series of elements—a deliverable, resources, leverages, focus, positions, display, and cash flow; (2) by a choice of product or service differentiation as unique, strong or weak specialty, or commodity; and (3) by developing sufficient sources of profit from innovation, rent, various forms of distribution, brokerage, insurance, financing, storage, and other services. Business strategies are assembled in the same way but have the added consideration of the nature of the total product line or sales package and the financial viability of the business unit.

Enterprise strategies are different; they deal with the overall nature of the organization and of the businesses in which it will engage. Leadership, opportunity, people, public, and resource strategies are the building blocks and desirability, managing, belonging, credibility, and payoff choice criteria govern the flow of management decisions. Enterprise-level strategies have received relatively little conscious attention in many organizations, and in the absence of specific guidance an organization transforms the actions of its managers into implicit policies to govern future action. Thus many enterprise-level strategies limit the performance of businesses and products sufficiently to establish areas in which the enterprise cannot be profitable.

Product or service, business, and enterprise strategies are the primary strategies, so named because they direct business actions. The functioning of an organization also requires large numbers of support strategies for the functions, divisions, or other organizational units to assist them in directing their action to support the product or service, business, and enterprise strategies dependent on their efforts. Few product (primary) strategies could succeed without a suitable marketing (support) strategy and most primary strategies have specific support requirements for their success.

FOUNDATIONS FOR STRATEGY

The chance of designing a successful strategy is greatly increased by a clear understanding of the fundamentals on which its design depends. Three basic areas are those defined by the nature of the product or service, of the market and competition, and of the business itself. The fundamentals of the product or service itself are established by its characteristics and by the choice of elements, degrees of differentiation, and sources of profit. The fundamentals of the market depend on its nature, position in its life cycle, and structure and also on the number, nature, and personality of the competitors. The fundamentals of the business include its learning-curve position in key functions, its stage of development in the business life cycle, its relative strength and market position, and its portfolio position in relation to the needs and contributions of any other businesses being managed by the same enterprise.

These fundamentals are not independent and many but not all are controlled by the management of the enterprise; that is, although the choice among the elements of strategy cannot be independent of the underlying nature of the product, there are many alternative ways to develop the same product potential, and the choices made there interact with market and business fundamentals. In the same way, the market life cycle, structure, and competition are initially determined by external forces but are ultimately influenced by the actions and responses of each major factor in the market; for example, when RCA changed the life-cycle characteristics of the television market by its heavy investments in color television and Warner-Lambert changed the mouthwash market when it shifted Listerine to a much higher level of advertising and promotion. These same major decisions changed the characteristics of the individual businesses offering these products; therefore the initial classifications of any existing product, market, and business situation are only tentative and subject to impact by the strategic choices and actions of the market participants.

DESIGNING EFFECTIVE STRATEGIES

In putting all of the enterprise, product, market, and business characteristics together with mission and goals and setting out to design a strategy, several basic characteristics of the business process need consideration. In the first place, many of the behavior patterns of a given business area are determined by custom and habit; although there are laws and regulations, in most cases they deal with only the smaller part of the total behavior pattern and business managers determine the rest. The managers of any business enjoy great freedom to change to different behavior patterns, and the opportunity to make up new rules if they can find rule patterns acceptable to their customers and market and beneficial to their own businesses. Making up new rules—for distribution patterns, terms of trade, basic relationships between suppliers, manufacturers, and customers—is one of the most creative and most potent strategy options. It is usually a difficult option because shifting market and customers to new behavior patterns is a cultural change process, not easy to accomplish but potentially rewarding.

Another strategy design option or even requirement is the creation of key resources necessary to attain the desired ends. Resources are not predetermined and constant, or obtained only from banks. What resources are really required to make a strategy work? What resources really control the effectiveness of that strategy and the profit levels that will result? Often the requirements lists include items such as credibility, capability, and efficiency which can exist only if management somehow creates them. Many of the key resources a business needs can be created as needed; many are available only through such creation; and in many cases these created resources are much more important than the resources bought with dollars. Resource creation is not always easy. It may be very difficult and may require a high order of management ability but it may also be the key to whether a strategy has a chance of success.

When Medi + Physics began to offer short-lived isotopes for hospital diagnostic testing, it wanted to persuade hospitals to stop making their own reagents for these purposes. To succeed it had to make the reagents during the night, standardize, test them to the satisfaction of the Food and Drug Administration, release them, and deliver them in the morning for use later that day; because of their short half-life, those not used that day had to be discarded. Medi + Physics had to create the capability of reliably manufacturing, testing, and delivering quality reagents on a rigid schedule and credibility at the hospitals that would cause them to discontinue their own less efficient reagent manufacture and schedule procedures and patients in anticipation that Medi + Physics would deliver quality materials on time. The created resources represented by the manufacturing and delivery capability and credibility at the hospitals were more critical to the success of the business than any of its other resources.

Making up rules and creating resources requires specific capabilities for successful execution, first from the management that devises the strategy, determines the timetable required, and directs the successful action. Often the capabilities, credibility, and efficiency requirements relate to characteristics of the organization that management chooses to build, and different levels of organizational effectiveness can be achieved. Many strategies require a high level of organizational effectiveness or gain substantially in their profitability by achieving it. To build a high level of organizational effectiveness requires a coherence and internal integrity in the human organization that substantially conditions management's enterprise strategy choices. Chapter 7 discussed the requirements of the excellence model, a prototype for the construction of a high-effectiveness organization. Firms that have made conflicting enterprise strategy choices cannot build this effectiveness and will not succeed if they choose strategies that require it.

The strategy design process makes use of created resources and new rules as appropriate, but the cutting edge is in the design and choice of the leverages that become the driving force for customer action and the needs-leverages linkages created from them. A proposed strategy, however, may be disabled or rejected if incompatible with organizational barriers and requirements and is unlikely to be designed successfully unless the designers have a clear understanding of the total environment in which the strategy will be operated; the perils of strategic blindness were discussed in Chapter 9. Strategies can be tested in various ways before they are put into action. A simple and effective strategic modeling technique was discussed in Chapter 8.

STRATEGIC ACTION AND CONTROL

For the desired flow, from planning and strategy to action, strategy and its design must be incorporated into a strategic management process (Figure 17.1). Strategic control, which requires a strategic overview for effective execution, concerns itself with the functioning of the key elements and in particular with the enterprise choice criteria. It should be coupled with a plan and program for managing the social impact of decisions, managing opportunity,

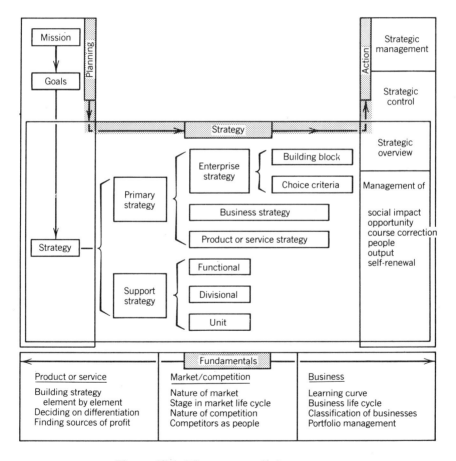

Figure 17.1. The strategy design process.

and avoiding regulatory and other pitfalls. Management of the people and operations is equally important, and a program for keeping the organization vital, effective, and current with new needs is essential. Together these issues add up to strategic management in which strategy design is coupled with effective execution and control and the firm can succeed and grow.

APPENDIX

PROFILE OF A PLAN[1]

One of the characteristics of the planning process is its pervasiveness. When major operations are being carried out under the direction of a management, planning is occurring and this planning follows a general framework. Although sometimes this planning may be disorganized or uncoordinated, the underlying process has a common trend.

OUTLINE OF A STRATEGIC PLAN

To aid in recognizing the general characteristics of this underlying process and applying them to a particular planning problem Figure A.1 is a useful outline. Although different outlines may be

[1]Adapted from George C. Sawyer, *Corporate Planning As A Creative Process* (Oxford, Ohio: Planning Executives Institute, 1983), pp. 10–19.

1. Executive summary

2. Background

3. Environment

4. Business appraisal

5. Mission

6. Goals

7. Strategy

8. Product or service programs

9. Forecast

10. Functional plans

11. Resource requirements

12. Financial analysis

13. Realism

14. Alternatives

15. Recommendations

Figure A.1. Outline of a strategic plan.

used, these same elements will be found in some form in any good strategic plan.

Executive Summary

Each plan should start with a brief section designed to give the essence of the plan and its recommendation in capsule form for the busy reader. At first the concept of a summary section is disturbing to some managers who would prefer that the reader be led through a logical sequence as the plan is constructed. Good literary and dramatic form call for careful articulation of the argument, a good flow of logic, and even an element of suspense before the final capsule of the plan is unfolded.

Real-world executives often lose patience with good literary presentation. To save time for accomplishment managers curtail reading time. Some follow the practice advocated by the late President Kennedy of skimming briefly to decide whether a document is worth reading. Others simply try a page or two and then reconsider. If the subject is not personally important or if the first pages have not caught his or her interest, the executive goes on to other things and the plan is shelved or discarded.

It is strongly recommended that any plan start with a brief summary. The larger part of the readership will never go beyond the summary, which should contain the substance of what they need to know. Then those few who have an interest or something at stake will read the plan carefully. They may read it as a means of learning about the business, as the basis for their approval, as a means of preparing a brief in its support, or as critical opponents searching for flaws. The body of a good plan will receive serious and critical readership but only from a relatively small group of friends and enemies. This body should be substantial if it is to withstand analysis and honestly supportive of the statements the summary contains.

Background

This is an important section too often omitted because a plan starts from a context that grows out of the history of the enterprise. The firm is controlled by managers with individual personalities; some have taken positions on issues and in any ongoing management processes a history of successes and failures is already established. The purpose of a background section in the plan is to state briefly the context in which the plan is being constructed and presented. This is a point of departure, with a set of assumptions about where the business has been and the stresses and strains that must be considered in planning the next steps.

One of the important things about a background section is that not all of the readers will agree with it. If a manager feels that his planning is heavily constrained by the need to make use of available plant capacity, it is important to say so. If shortage of cash requires delay in previous plans for increasing inventories, it should be stated. If these assumptions are not stated, the chance to reinforce or to change them may be missed. If members of the management group that is reviewing the plan disagree with these assumptions, they can say so and perhaps new programs will become possible.

In any case it is important to state this context, to refresh the memories of those who may not have thought about this business as an entity since the last plan was presented. Thus each reader will start the plan with an awareness of the boundaries and limitations used by the planning group and built into the structure.

Environment

Each plan also has a surrounding context. Businesses are affected by recessions, earthquakes, wars, disasters, social stress, market conditions, competitive actions, inflation, taxes, and a host of other external factors. Obvious though many of these factors may be, they are often missed by managers so involved in the day-to-day routine that they have no time to stop and think about the world in which their business functions. A brief section on environment provides the discipline of an organized statement in a context appropriate to the plan.

In a strategic plan the environment section should survey the environment briefly and comprehensively but should only devote time to careful development where a particular factor is likely to affect corporate decisions now or in the near future. A survey of environmental factors often starts with likely impacts on the business of developments in the political and regulatory environment, of social forces and economic trends, of changing technology, and of developments in the competitive environment. Also it often includes a profile of the actual markets in which the business operates. In some cases the ecological factors that influence the business require separate discussion. As its contribution to the plan the environment section highlights the most critical sensitivities and vulnerabilities of the business to the world around it.

Business Appraisal

This short section summarizes the business situation. Given the background as stated and the present and projected environment as the planning group sees it, what is a realistic assessment of the business outlook? The purpose of the appraisal section is to sharpen and converge the analysis drawn out of the background and environment and to underscore those key questions that provide a backdrop for the plan to follow.

Mission

The mission is a statement of the role in which a business plans to serve society. As a profit-seeking entity, a business unit can survive only by providing goods or services to some segment of society at a price greater than the cost. For the necessary price to be paid the purchasers must see value in the purchase greater than the purchasing power that must be surrendered to obtain them. The business must perform some valuable role by offering goods or services in which buyers see value greater than the cost or it cannot survive. This role, in which it can find the basis for its pursuit of profit, is its mission.

Although the mission of a business may be derived more or less spontaneously during its early struggles, that mission or franchise must be thoroughly understood and be changed only intentionally and with care, lest the commercial basis of success be undermined in some expansion.

Goals

Goals—or objectives—are a necessary precursor to any serious plan for accomplishment. These goals may be informal or formal. When the management of an enterprise has been informal in the past, the planning group will often find that goals have never been made explicit. Often one of the major benefits of a more organized planning process is that members of the organization are led to recognize and share a statement of their goals for the first time.

To reemphasize: a plan is action laid out in advance. The action is aimed at accomplishment. A statement of what the business is trying to accomplish is a statement of its goals. If goals cannot be found and stated, there is hardly any point in trying to plan action.

The mission is a statement of the service to society for which the business is designed, and the goals are specific ends to be achieved by business action. Here, and in any plan, goals occur in hierarchy, where the highest level is the statement of overall accomplishment that is being attempted. One business may strive to increase market share, and another may set its goals in terms of sales and profits. The Avis "we try harder" campaign carried with it a clear-cut goal of challenging Hertz and becoming number one instead of number two in the car rental business. At one point the Anheuser-Busch organization drove itself to increase its output to a billion barrels of beer.

The purpose of a goals section in a plan is to draw out a concise statement of what the following programs of action are designed to accomplish. This makes the logic much clearer to the executives who must approve the plan and helps the planning group itself to clarify that logic.

Strategy

From a set of goals which is often somewhat abstract the next step is to their means of achievement. Given that market share is to be increased, how should this be done? Among the several alternatives, is the best option a major promotion campaign? A different method of distribution? A radical price cut? From these and still other alternatives a basic approach to goal achievement must be selected for the planning to proceed. This major approach is the strategy this business will follow in striving to achieve its goals.

Strategy as a term comes from the military and the analogy between a business plan and a battle plan has often been elaborated. Just as in planning the conquest of France the German general staff defined a series of alternative strategies and prepared a complete battle plan for each strategy before making its choice, it is often necessary to consider the results that various business alternatives might yield before a specific strategy can be chosen and put in motion.

Product or Service Programs

When a strategy has been selected the next step is to block out the major action areas around which the implementation plans should be organized. These often represent groups of products or services, hence the term product or service programs. It is common to find that products in a product line occur in families which should be logically related in their planning and marketing more than other products in the line; for example, in a mail order catalog from Sears or Montgomery-Ward the products are grouped together. The buying staff can plan for appliances, televisions, power tools, or women's shoes as groups of products in such a line.

In moving from strategy to forecasted accomplishments the forecasting can best be organized in a logical framework built on natural relationships. Definition of these natural relationships as the basis for product programs is a useful prelude to forecasting, and aids in developing a consistent set of actions to implement the chosen strategy.

Forecast

From the product or service programs developed from the strategy, what will the output be? In a strategic plan for a business selling products or services the forecast is for sales or other revenues. This is based on the number of units that will be sold and the price that will be charged. When products are leased or installed on a shared-revenue basis the terms of the forecast may be somewhat different. In any case, the forecast section is intended as a simple statement of the revenue that the business can be expected to generate as a result of the plan presented here for approval.

Functional Plans

The strategy, as broken into product programs and developed into a forecast, is a projection of results that can be achieved only if the necessary components of the organization function together in a coordinated way. This means that each of the functional areas with a role in implementing the strategy must itself develop a plan for this role with its own set of goals and strategy. This section of the strategic plan is intended to present these functional plans in relation to the strategy and forecast.

Detailed functional planning is often necessary. The corresponding component of the strategic plan, whether it be for marketing, manufacturing, distribution, research, engineering or another function, is usually limited to a brief summary supported elsewhere by a separate plan elaborated to the required extent. Production plans often are carried out in great detail, but the strategic plan need contain only a brief summary integrated with the related functional efforts.

Resource Requirements

The functional plans become real and meaningful to management only when they also are related to a statement of what the effort will cost. If an expanded program requires more people, new capital commitments, or some other change in resource needs the resource requirements section will show this as well as the planned use of existing resources. The resource requirements of all of the functional plans should add together to a statement of total resources required to accomplish the strategic plan that is being presented.

The resource requirements section will be cast largely in

financial terms but it is useful also to include other statements of the demands on scarce resources; for instance, many managements find it useful to have a tabulation of the numbers and levels of people required to staff each function or the loading on a key item of equipment.

Financial Analysis

From the resource requirements, which show a full statement of the costs of the business, and from the forecast, which projects its revenues, an income statement and balance sheet can be constructed and examined. The financial analysis section is intended to present and analyze this income statement and balance sheet in terms of rates of return, resource demands, and general soundness of the approach. Often the first analysis of a new plan shows that it is less than satisfactory and a reappraisal of forecasts and use of resources is required before the plan can be completed and submitted.

Realism

A plan is of necessity built on assumptions which should be chosen with care and presented as made. At the end of the planning process it is useful to the group doing the planning and to those who must approve the results if the composite of those assumptions is reviewed for realism.

The planning group should not be allowed to make assumptions and then disclaim them, but, given that the best assumptions have been made at every stage, there is still room for a composite judgment as to whether the probabilities of a plan working out well are good or bad because of the risk of outside events interfering with its progress. The purpose of this realism section is to give the next levels of management an appraisal from the planning group, particularly when others will raise these same uncertainties as issues. For control of the discussion process it is best to identify and address known uncertainties openly, to show that they have been considered, and to present them from the perspective that the planning group prefers to use.

Alternatives

Almost every strategy and almost every plan is based on a choice among alternatives. The normal human process is to seize immediately on the alternative that seems best, but in establishing the credibility of a plan it is important to establish that other alternatives are known to exist and have been considered. The purpose of an alternatives section is to catalog some of them briefly and to mention the reasons for their discard. Often a proposed course of action is strengthened by this review because of the unpalatability of the other alternatives.

Another part of the value of an alternatives section is to reduce the psychological pressure on top management that a good, well-presented plan may tend to create. The thrust of a strong plan toward the chosen alternative may be so powerful that it will create resistance as management begins to feel as if its approval were being demanded. It is useful to remind top management that there are choices, that they are not being "forced" to approve the plan, although the other courses of action may be less attractive. This review of alternatives helps top management to become more comfortable with the strategy and recommendations of a good plan and moves these managers toward its approval.

Recommendations

The energy and exposure required in laying out a plan and circulating it to top management is a part of a program for accomplishment. The plan should be a means to obtaining top management's endorsement of the action program. The recommendation section summarizes briefly the specific actions that should be taken and requests approval. If the plan has been well constructed these recommendations, which were presented briefly in the executive summary, will have developed from the logic of the plan and will stand out as good candidates for executive approval when the plan is reviewed.

BUILDING A SIMPLE PLAN OUTLINE

The preceding section has presented 15 elements that a strategic plan should include. Most other plans should also include them. These elements were presented in a natural order and could become 15 chapters, but this direct application would often be too formal or stereotyped.

Although major planning documents are produced in many corporations and these 15 elements form a logical, well-balanced, and effective structure for a substantive literary effort, the theme here is to minimize formality and to give extra emphasis to those elements most useful to a specific management at a specific time. In many cases a short, well-conceived plan will fit the need better than a massive work and the savings are very great. A good, short plan is more likely to be read and used and as such is better able to return the value on which the value-added planning process must be justified.

The point is that the 15 elements cited here can easily be combined in a number of ways and should be when it would help to achieve a briefer and more effective presentation. Functional plans and resource requirements or missions and goals can often be discussed together, but the discipline of carrying out planning effectively requires that the concept of each element be adequately included, even though no formal chapter heading may be necessary.

THE PLANNING PROCESS AS A CONTINUOUS FLOW

The planning process is a continuum and even a segmentation into 15 elements is somewhat artificial. The nature of planning is such that the analysis of the issues and synthesis of possible solutions must often move through these elements again and again before the projected profits and returns can have the best possible relationship with inputs and investments.

The planning process is a flow process that cycles through its various articulations as decisions occur, sales are made, and new facts are gathered. As such the planning process is an essential component of the management operating system and should be made to flow as simply and naturally as possible.

The planning process also produces plans. A plan can be visualized as a snapshot of this process, based on the relationship between the elements of the business at one moment in time and projecting the evolution of this relationship into the future. Just as different snapshots of two friends in conversation may differ substantially in details as the conversation progresses, so may two plans developed from the same process for the same business at different times. A well-conceived plan defines directions and general relationships, and under all but the most turbulent conditions these relationships should change very slowly. However, the details of a specific plan are usually misleading to some degree because these details were determined by special conditions in that moment when the snapshot was taken. Thus plans tend to be most effective in defining strategies and general principles of action and least effective in predicting or controlling the details of actions to be taken at some moment in the future.

SUMMARY

In the general case all plans are analogs in that there is a context, goals are necessary as are a strategy and a set of actions, all with forecasted results and projected costs. As these are balanced, they lead to outcome analysis and recommendations for action. The outline presented here is for a strategic plan but it has a general applicability. In some planning problems, however, different sections will need more or less development and must fit the process of the business; for example, in some activities in which the output is not quantitative the forecast must be in qualitative terms.

Planning is a process with a logical sequence of elements that should be reflected in any good plan. The foregoing outline represents one way in which these elements can be put together in a useful and constructive way.

INDEX